PRAISE FOR
RELATIONAL INTELLIGENCE

No success story is written alone, and nothing significant is achieved in a silo. Whether you recognize it or not, your relationships shape your future. That's why Dharius Daniels's new book, *Relational Intelligence*, is a read you shouldn't miss.

Steven Furtick, pastor of Elevation Church
and *New York Times* bestselling author

Pastor Dharius Daniels is undeniably one of the most brilliant minds of this time. Though there are hundreds of books centered on relationships, Pastor Daniels veers into an uncharted territory on the subject of relational intelligence. In this masterful exposition, the dire need of people skills is taught in a way that incites transformative thinking. As you journey through the pages, you are compelled to consider that the fulfillment of one's purpose swings on the ability to establish healthy human connections. This is more than another good read; it is a revolution in book form.

Tasha Cobbs Leonard, Grammy Award–winning
worship pastor and leader

Relationships. Everything in our lives is rooted in that one word. Lives are expanded or contracted based on how we navigate relationships. Dr. Dharius Daniels provides insight, wisdom, and practical tools to maximize both our horizontal relationships and our vertical one. When people are properly positioned in our lives, true fruit can be produced. When God is prioritized in our lives, legacy can be established. I have watched the life of my friend Dharius Daniels and can attest that the authority of his words stems from the example he walks out daily. His voice is essential in today's diluted culture that diminishes relationships to a mere swipe to the left. This book is a course correction for those of us willing to apply its truths.

John Gray, pastor of Relentless Church

We know God's desire is for us to be in unity with one another, but in *Relational Intelligence*, Dr. Dharius charges us to take this to the next level. If we want to be obedient to all that God has called us to, we need more than a body with a pulse to walk through life with. To go the distance with purpose, we need people in our lives who inspire us to carry out our God-given calling. This book will help you define, discern, align, and assess relationships in your life.

Levi Lusko, lead pastor of Fresh Life Church
and bestselling author

I've found that at the core of most of life's challenges is our inability to categorize and cultivate the right relationships. The way Dharius Daniels is able to articulate with such practicality how to manage such a difficult area of our lives is so refreshing. It's a blueprint to health and stability in all of our interactions with people. I'm so glad he wrote this book!

Sheryl Brady, pastor of The Potter's House North
and author of *Don't Miss the Moment*

Dharius Daniels knows that successful, healthy relationships rely on spiritual wisdom and diligent practice. He shares how our interactions with others influence every area of our lives—including our faith. With straight-up wisdom from God's Word, as well as insight into our longings for connection, Dharius outlines specific ways to improve, enrich, and enhance the way we relate to others. *Relational Intelligence* is the book we all wish we had read sooner!

Chris Hodges, senior pastor of Church of the Highlands
and author of *The Daniel Dilemma*

As a physician, I'm in the "serving people" business, and relational intelligence is an often underappreciated trait to help us be effective. In this incredible book, Dr Dharius Daniels masterfully teaches the reader about life, life's moving parts, and how to make sense of it all to better fulfill our individual purpose while lifting up God at the same time. Every paragraph and every line hit home. And you will absolutely leave this book more edified and more in command of your own relational intelligence—a vital key to your success!

Myron L. Rolle, MD MSc, Harvard Neurosurgery,
former NFL player, Rhodes Scholar

Relational
INTELLIGENCE

Relational INTELLIGENCE

THE PEOPLE SKILLS YOU NEED FOR
THE LIFE OF PURPOSE YOU WANT

DR. DHARIUS DANIELS

ZONDERVAN

Relational Intelligence
Copyright © 2020 by Dharius Daniels

Requests for information should be addressed to:
Zondervan, *3900 Sparks Dr. SE, Grand Rapids, Michigan 49546*

Zondervan titles may be purchased in bulk for educational, business, fundraising, or promotional use. For information, please email SpecialMarkets@Zondervan.com.

ISBN 978-0-310-35785-8 (audio)

Library of Congress Cataloging-in-Publication Data

Name: Daniels, Dharius, 1979- author.
Title: Relational intelligence : the people skills you need for the life of purpose you want / Dharius Daniels.
Description: Grand Rapids : Zondervan, 2020. | Includes bibliographical references. | Summary: "Relational Intelligence by Dr. Dharius Daniels is your guide to increasing your relational skills so that you can accomplish your purpose, advance your career, and improve the spiritual, physical, and emotional quality of your life"-- Provided by publisher.
Identifiers: LCCN 2019034818 (print) | LCCN 2019034819 (ebook) | ISBN 9780310357827 (hardcover) | ISBN 9780310357841 (ebook)
Subjects: LCSH: Interpersonal relations—Religious aspects—Christianity. | Friendship—Religious aspects—Christianity.
Classification: LCC BV4597.52 .D36 2020 (print) | LCC BV4597.52 (ebook) | DDC 248.4—dc23
LC record available at https://lccn.loc.gov/2019034818
LC ebook record available at https://lccn.loc.gov/2019034819

Published in association with Dupree Miller & Associates, 4311 Oak Lawn Avenue, #650, Dallas, TX 75219.

Cover design: Micah Kandros
Cover illustration: artway / Shutterstock
Interior design: Kait Lamphere

Printed in the United States of America

22 23 24 25 26 27 28 29 /LSC/ 15 14 13 12 11 10

To the most transformative relationship in my life—Jesus—
following your life and leadership
was the most intelligent decision I've ever made.

To the most significant relationships in my life—
my wife, Shameka, and my two children, Seth and Gabriel—
your presence in my life is a constant reminder
of God's love for me.

Finally, to the ultimate teammate and friend, Ramone Harper—
who transitioned to heaven before this book was released—
this book and so much more in my life and ministry
wouldn't be possible without you.
I know you are watching from heaven.

Thank you for showing me that when the dust settles,
what matters most are the people who love you the best.
I dedicate this book to you.

EPIGRAPH

Walk with the wise and become wise,
for a companion of fools suffers harm.

Proverbs 13:20

CONTENTS

PART 4: Assessing Your Relationships

FOREWORD

None of us were born being nice. No offense intended, but we started out this life ill-mannered and innately selfish, and we had to pick up on social rules and etiquette over the course of time. We had to learn to "use our words" as opposed to screaming for what we wanted. We had to learn to say "please" instead of "mine." We had to learn that it's not okay to bite your friends. We had to learn how to communicate, resolve conflicts, negotiate, forgive, give and receive, and a myriad of other social abilities. In other words, we had to learn people skills.

The good news is that people skills are just that—*skills*. We aren't talking about some mysterious, mythical ability that God has granted to a few special personality types, while the rest of us are doomed to loneliness or broken friendships. We are talking about a skill set that anyone can, and everyone should, develop over the course of their lives, because we will never reach a place where we no longer need people.

Real relationships matter *a lot*. People make us or break us. They lift us up or pull us down. One evening of laughter with the right people can refresh our souls and lift our spirits.

One conversation with the right mentor can alter the course of our careers. One romantic relationship with the right person can lead to a life of passion, companionship, and intimacy. The older I get, the more convinced I am that the greatest resource we have is not our money, our time, our careers, or our talents—it's the people in our lives.

If there's one thing social media illustrates, it's that you can have thousands of friends and yet still be lonely. That's not cynicism: it's just reality. We all know that friends, fans, and followers don't necessarily translate to real relationships. Social media has its place, but the human soul longs for an intimate connection with specific individuals. We all want to know and be known, to love and be loved. In a world that is becoming more connected, more informed, and more public by the day, close friends matter to a greater degree than ever.

If relationships are that important, then our ability to identify, form, grow, and sustain friendships is crucial. That's the premise of the book you're about to read. My good friend Dharius Daniels calls this *relational intelligence*, and it's all about getting good at being with people.

It's worth noting, in conclusion, that the reason relationships matter so much is that *people* matter. The goal of becoming people-smart is not to get the most out of others. It's not to manipulate our way to the top. It's to *be* a better friend and to *have* better friends. It's to give the most we can to others, and to do so in a reciprocal context—an environment where we give and receive and give again. Life is better together, so let's get better at this thing called "together."

Judah Smith,
New York Times bestselling author

INTRODUCTION

Your greatest gifts walk into
your life on two legs.

What you're holding in your hands is more than a compilation of pages filled with information; it is a crucial and consequential conversation. It is a dialogue about your destiny. It is a pep talk about purpose. It is a communiqué about your calling.

You are probably thinking, *Wait, I thought this book was about relationships!* You are absolutely right. It is. That said, relationships are about more than relationships; relationships are about your life. Therefore, relationship management is life management. Every single area of your life is inevitably impacted by your relationships. Your spiritual, physical, financial, emotional, and professional progress is tied and tethered to who you allow to be a part of and influence your life. Therefore, if you are serious about taking your life to the next level, you should be serious about taking your relationships to the next level.

One of the wisest men to have ever lived, King Solomon, put it this way in Proverbs 13:20: "Walk with the wise and become wise, for a companion of fools suffers harm." Solomon

13

suggests that we ultimately become like those we walk with. You may have heard it put another way: "Association breeds assimilation."

In other words, there is no such thing as a casual relationship. All relationships are consequential. They are catalytic. They push us forward or hold us back. They propel us into purpose or push us into pain. They bring joy or bring sorrow. They are incredibly impactful, even when we are unaware of their impact. Paul told the people of Corinth in 1 Corinthians 15:33, "Do not be misled: 'Bad company corrupts good character.'" I'd like to pose a question. Why would Paul warn the audience of this epistle to not be misled? Could it be because he understands that it is possible for us to be oblivious to the impact that our relationships have on our lives?

Paul must have understood something that I think is important for you and me to understand. Whether we realize it or not, our relationships are "purpose partners." Our purpose requires people. We never go just as far as our dream; we go as far as our *team*. We need more than people who simply provide us company; we need people who help us carry out our calling. We need more than a circle; we need a squad. Therefore, some people's presence in our lives are not accidents; they are expressions of God's providence.

God sends certain people into our lives in certain seasons for certain reasons. However, while God sends them, we must see them. God releases them, and we must recognize them. God assigns them, and we must align them. As a pastor, I often hear people say, "Well, Pastor, I don't need friends. God fulfills my every need." Absolutely. God does. But there are some needs he fulfills directly, and then there are other needs he fulfills indirectly. Is that not what happened in the Garden of Eden? God essentially said, "Even though I'm here, there's something Adam needs that's going to come in the form of a person."

Enter Eve. God creates Eve and sends her to Adam as a helper, but Adam also saw her that way and treated her accordingly.

When something is this consequential, we must be incredibly intentional and intelligent about how we manage it. I know you may not be accustomed to seeing the word *intelligence* associated with the word *relationships*. However, I'd contend that if there is anything we need to be intelligent about, it's our relationships. As Jim Collins writes in his book *Good to Great*, we need the right people on our bus and we also need them in the right seats.[1] Everyone in our lives has a place, and we must put them there.

This book will help you figure out what that looks like.

If you're serious about success and passionate about purpose, you must be intentional about putting the people in your lives—the ones currently there and the ones to come—in the right places. I want to show you how to live with RQ— relational intelligence.

WHAT IS RQ?

You may have heard of IQ and EQ, but RQ is equally as important. Relational intelligence is the ability to discern if someone should be a part of our lives and what place they should occupy, and then align them accordingly. It's the ability to appropriately define and align our relationships. This may be difficult to hear, but although everyone should be loved appropriately and valued equally, they should be treated differently. I imagine you are probably thinking we should treat *everyone* right. If you are a person of faith, then you are likely thinking we are *all* created in God's image and have equal worth and value. Therefore, shouldn't we treat *everyone* the same?

Here is my faith-filled, biblically influenced, prayerfully considered answer: No, we shouldn't. Yes, we should treat everyone right, but treating everyone right doesn't mean we treat everyone the same. Jesus didn't. Relating to people properly should not be confused with treating them equally.

As a pastor who has the privilege of getting a behind-the-scenes view of thousands of lives, I can say with great conviction that it's not just important to have the right *people* in your life, but it's also important to have them in the right *place*. Having people in the wrong place can cause things that should be held in confidence to get exposed, bad advice and counsel to be adhered to, and destiny to be impacted.

This principle not only applies to people's personal lives, but it is equally relevant when it comes to leadership. Hiring the right team member, managing the right team member, and releasing the wrong team member all require relational intelligence. There is no area of our lives that is unaffected by our RQ.

Our IQ and EQ affect and impact our RQ. There have been lots of conversations recently regarding the significance of EQ, or emotional intelligence. Emotional intelligence, as defined by the researchers who coined the term, Peter Salovey and John Mayer, is "the ability to monitor one's own and others' feelings and emotions, to discriminate among them and to use this information to guide one's thinking and actions."[2] EQ is important, but it's only one part of a larger equation when it comes to relationships. Consider this: IQ (intellectual capacity, ability to reason) + EQ (emotional capacity/intelligence) = RQ (relational intelligence). As you can see, the ability to recognize and manage our emotions that comes with EQ, combined with the ability to reasonably assess our lives and relationships (IQ), creates the strong possibility that we will develop the people skills we need for the life of purpose we want.

IMPERFECT, BUT POWERFUL

This book is not about finding perfect relationships. I can help you with that right now—they don't exist! In her book *The Gifts of Imperfection*, Brené Brown writes, "Understanding the difference between healthy striving and perfectionism is critical to laying down the shield [the ways we protect ourselves] and picking up your life. Research shows that perfectionism hampers success. In fact, it's often the path to depression, anxiety, addiction, and life-paralysis."[3] As applicable as this is to us individually, it's increasingly important to remember when it comes to our relationships.

There are no perfect relationships, and looking for them is not only unhealthy but also unbiblical. I think it's important to understand that our relationships don't have to be perfect to be powerful. The best relationships are inundated with obstacles, challenges, and roadblocks.

The goal of this book is to offer some insight and guidance to help you develop impactful relationships, although they will be imperfect. In order to accomplish this task, we should consult the ultimate relationship expert—God. To be clear, the most intelligent way to approach relationships is God's way. I believe this because God is the inventor of relationships. He created the first relationship. I believe the creator of a thing is the one who gets to determine how to get the best use out of it. The inventor of a thing is the best one to give instructions on how to best use it. So, bottom line? Relationships are God's idea, and God knows the best way to manage them and has revealed this way in Scripture.

Scripture gives us a blueprint for the way relationships should be managed, and this blueprint helps us construct and grow relationships that are fruitful. The Bible offers an architectural plan of sorts that helps us construct the kind of relationships that God models for us in the Trinity. The Father, Son, and Holy Spirit have a unity that's incredibly productive, and we can have the same thing.

You don't have to live lonely, broken, battered, and bruised. I'm not sure if you are aware of this, but I believe that many people are settling for less than God's best in the area of their relationships. Many don't have the right people in their life at all, and others may not have the right people in the right place. I believe we don't have to settle. I believe we don't have to place a period where God wants a comma. It doesn't matter what season of life you are in. I believe God wants to send you some friends, associates, assignments, and advisors to walk with you on the remainder of your life's journey. You will be ready for them if you are willing to raise your RQ.

ONE MORE WORD

I recognize that some of the categorizations and analyses I offer in this book may sound a bit rigid. You may even find yourself thinking that this approach is not organic enough. *Shouldn't we just let our relationships do what they're going to do? Go with the flow?* For some, it's over the top, and for others, it's even unnecessary. But when I was growing up, there was a board game we used to play a lot—Monopoly. To win, you have to buy, sell, negotiate, or otherwise strategically acquire certain properties. But the most critical part of your success in Monopoly is the way you roll the dice. And unless you're a cheater, you can't control how you roll the dice.

Having your success based on a roll of the dice is one thing, but it is not the way God intended for us to live our lives. Unfortunately, rolling the dice is the way too many of us make relationship decisions. No strategy, no intelligence, and all feeling. We manage no other area of life that way. We don't roll the dice at work; we build plans and set goals.

Isn't your life more consequential? Your purpose is too necessary. Your contribution to the earth is too needed for it to be jeopardized or compromised because you won't take your relationships seriously. And without a doubt, relationships are serious. They make us or break us. They push us forward, or they pull us back. They catapult us higher, or they keep us lower. They are the singular greatest source of joy and peace in people's lives.

We owe it to ourselves; we owe it to the God who created us; and we owe it to the people who are depending on us to manage this area of our life well—because the skill needed to manage relationships is a life skill. If we commit to developing this skill, we can have the relationships we need for the life of purpose we want.

PART 1

Defining Your Relationships

Greater love has no one than this:
to lay down one's life for one's friends.
John 15:13

The question of how we define and categorize each of our relationships may seem like a trivial one, but it is an indispensable task. And I get it! As believers, it feels wrong—maybe even unbiblical—to place people in categories. It may feel like we are assigning importance to one person over another. But as we dive into this section of the book, we'll see that it's not the case at all! Without defining the relationships in our lives, we cannot effectively accomplish our purpose. As Jesus outlined in John 15:13, part of our purpose is to be a relational asset— not a liability—in the lives of the people God sends to us. It's impossible to align a relationship we haven't defined. So let's start there! Let's define what categories exist and what they mean for us and the people in our lives.

Category #1
FRIENDS

Friend.

We use that word too loosely. Too flippantly. We use it too generously. And most damaging of all, we give the title to people who haven't earned it. I recognize that using the word *earn* makes some folks nervous. It implies a kind of quid pro quo. It can feel icky. So let me be clear. Yes, God has called us to love. A person doesn't have to earn our love if we call ourselves believers. But I'm not talking about love; I'm talking about friendship. It's different. Remember Jesus in John 15?

> "Greater love has no one than this: to lay down one's life for one's friends. You are my friends if you do what I command. I no longer call you servants, because a servant does not know his master's business. Instead, I have called you friends, for everything that I learned from my Father I have made known to you."
>
> *John 15:13–15*

Don't miss the point here. He says if somebody's your friend, you give them your *life*. Coworkers, clients, and anyone may get your life resources—your talents and your time. As a spiritual leader, coach, and teacher, I don't even have to know you to offer and utilize my gifts for you. But in order for you to get *me*, for me to "make known to you" all the intimate things God has shared with me, you must be my friend. However, friends get your life. They get access to you in different ways and influence you in different degrees. In other words there is a difference between giving your life to someone and spending your life with someone.

Jesus breaks it down. He says in verse 14, "You are my friends if you do what I command" and in verse 15, he says, "I no longer call you servants because a servant does not know his master's business." Jesus is saying to the disciples, "We just shifted our relationship from what it was, to friendship. Full stop. Jesus makes this statement to some people but not all people. He made it to those who had walked with him long enough to demonstrate that this moniker applies.

Understanding this distinction is crucial to us embracing the concepts I will present in this book. We must be good at defining and stewarding our relationships. As the apostle Paul said, "we owe no man anything but to love him" (see Romans 13:8). We only owe people love. We don't owe people access to our life.

Friendship was and is God's idea. It is one of the ways he meets a significant desire of all our hearts. God's greatest gifts often walk into our lives on two legs. Friends are individuals who are relational assets and not liabilities. Friends are those whom God escorts into our environments because there is something they need to be for us in order to help us be what we need to be for him. Friends offer more than company; they help us carry out our calling.

A TRUE FRIEND, INDEED

I was nineteen years old and a sophomore at Millsaps College in Jackson, Mississippi. At the time, I was on the brink of a bout with what I call situational depression. It wasn't clinical, but it was devastating just the same. I'd just experienced a series of consecutive events that I was simply not emotionally prepared to manage and process properly. I remember lying in bed all day, lights off, struggling to even make it to my classes. The only time I would get relief was when I went to church. There was a Bible study I would go to on Thursday nights in Jackson, and I was also part of a gospel choir at our school that had rehearsal on Tuesday nights.

I would go to Tuesday night rehearsals to get a brief respite from my sadness, but as soon as I walked out of there, the heaviness and negative emotions would overtake me. The darkness would descend and remain until I could make it to Thursday night Bible study.

Enter Terrance Alexander.

I met him through a mutual friend who was actually one of my best friends. My friend would go on and on about his experience with Terrance. In light of how I felt, I was completely open to, maybe even desperate for, help. One thing to note here is that my emotional troubles weren't resolved by simple church attendance or engaging in spiritual disciplines. Sometimes people feel as if being sad or going through tough times means they are somehow spiritually deficient or disingenuous. That's not true. I had a relationship with God, but I needed better relationships with people. If you find that statement problematic, consider this: In the creation narrative, God said it was not good for man to be alone. Why would God say something like that when Adam wasn't actually alone? God was there, right? We aren't our best selves just simply by our connections with God. We were also created to have healthy connections with others. I wasn't equipped with the tools I needed to cultivate those kinds of relationships. I would soon learn how.

I remember we first met on a weeknight. My friend Marcus had arranged the meeting, and although nervous, I went. Terrance was staying in a dorm on campus. I walked through the glass doors and swiped my ID card. As I entered the lobby, I noticed this unassuming young man seated at a table. I don't know if I was expecting somebody in a three-piece suit or just a super churchy dude, but he—with his T-shirt, jeans, and glasses—was very relaxed and easygoing. When I sat down at the table, I was certainly a bit guarded, yet, at the same time I was clear on one thing: I needed a friend.

Terrance asked some very engaging questions that first day. Different kinds of questions. Questions that communicated his genuine care for people generally and for me specifically. "How are you doing? How are you feeling?" he first asked. But then he delved deeper. Began probing my heart. "How's your relationship with God?" Each question exposed the areas in my spirit that were lacking.

I left that conversation—and subsequent ones—feeling like I would feel when I left choir rehearsal or Bible study—just straight up reinvigorated. It felt like I'd been revived. But Terrance offered me more than an emotional IV filled with hope—hope that would only wear off after I left him. I didn't just feel different after we hung out. He helped me think differently; he helped me see differently. My constant engagement with him led to me wrestling with some things on a consistent basis that ultimately caused me to shift my paradigm, develop a stronger relationship with God, and gain the emotional fortitude I needed to withstand the onslaught of traumas I was dealing with at the time. As a result of that friendship, I stepped into my call to ministry. I got more focused on my education, and my emotional, spiritual, and relational life improved dramatically.

Terrance Alexander was a clear demonstration of what friendship should look like. He showed me the kind of care and camaraderie that God intends us to have. I found my way back to joy through my friendship with him.

THE SEEING FACTOR

An important question we should ask ourselves is this: How do we recognize a Terrance in our lives? There are things that all of us want in a friendship. However, there are some things that we may not want but may actually need. For example, most of us want loyalty and acceptance. However, if the loyalty isn't biblical, it won't be beneficial. Allow me to use an example from the life of King David:

> In the morning David wrote a letter to Joab and sent it with Uriah. In it he wrote, "Put Uriah out in front where the fighting is fiercest. Then withdraw from him so he will be struck down and die."
> So while Joab had the city under siege, he put Uriah at a place where he knew the strongest defenders were. When the men of the city came out and fought against

Joab, some of the men in David's army fell; moreover, Uriah the Hittite died.

Joab sent David a full account of the battle.

2 Samuel 11:14–18

Joab helped David almost ruin his life in the name of loyalty. An unhealthy loyalty is one that is always committed to a person's wishes—what they *want*. But biblical loyalty is committing to a person's well-being—what they *need*. Sometimes what we want might destroy us, and if those we call friends are always loyal to what we want, they become an accessory to the destruction of our destinies. If someone wants to ruin their life, real friends don't offer their assistance.

So, you may be wondering, *What traits should I look for in friendships that reflect what God intends?* I'm glad you asked. There are a few significant characteristics we find in Scripture that should be helpful.

1. UNSHAKABLE CHARACTER

Do not be misled: "Bad company corrupts good character."

1 Corinthians 15:33

In his book *The People Factor*, Van Moody says there is no such thing as a neutral relationship.[4] Every relationship impacts you in some way. It either helps or hurts, builds up or tears down, brings you higher or lower. Proverbs 13:20 corroborates this claim: "Walk with the wise and become wise, for a companion of fools suffers harm."

Whoever walks with us in the present is deciding what's going to happen in the future. This is why friendship is so important. Friends help frame people's futures. Character matters. Their character becomes your crisis, and yours becomes theirs. You never have to worry about someone being jealous of you if they aren't the jealous type. You don't have to be concerned about being deceived if your friends aren't deceptive. You won't have to consider being misled if your friends have integrity. Why would you place your life in the hands of someone whose character is not consistent?

The only thing keeping their character issues from impacting you directly is their relationship with you, but if your relationship ends, it's entirely possible you will have to worry about the ramification of their character flaws and what they will do to you. If they don't do that "thing" to anyone, then you don't have to worry about them doing that "thing" to you, regardless of where the relationship goes. You need people as friends who have unshakable character.

So reflect on your current friendships. Do the people you call friends meet this criterion?

2. UNCONDITIONAL LOVE

A friend loves at all times,
and a brother is born for a time of adversity.

Proverbs 17:17

This is pretty well spelled out in this verse. Biblical love is not affection; it's activity. It is unconquerable benevolence. A commitment to seek my highest good. You have to handle the best of me and worst of me without changing how you deal with me. Henri Nouwen captures what this looks like in his book *Out of Solitude: Three Meditations on the Christian Life*:

When we honestly ask ourselves which persons in our lives mean the most to us, we often find that it is those who, instead of giving much advice, solutions, or cures, have chosen rather to share our pain and touch our wounds with a gentle and tender hand. The friend who can be silent with us in a moment of despair or confusion, who can stay with us in an hour of grief and bereavement, who can tolerate not-knowing, not-curing, not-healing and face with us the reality of our powerlessness, that is a friend who cares.[5]

This benevolence is the essence of unconditional love.

3. UNBRIDLED HONESTY

Wounds from a friend can be trusted,
but an enemy multiplies kisses.

Proverbs 27:6

Tell me the truth. We must love people enough to tell them the truth, even if it's a truth you haven't mastered and they don't want to hear it. The challenge is, if we honestly assess the relationships we have both within and outside the church, we discover that sometimes there is a lack of authenticity. This is quite the opposite of what true friendships should look like though.

Within our friendships, we should be able to be undeniably authentic. We should be able to say, "This is someone who really accepts me for me, and therefore I accept the truth they are telling me." Because an authentic friend would rather be willing to hurt my feelings than see me hurt my life. A friend may be the only person who can speak into my life truthfully because they are likely only one of a few who actually know what's going on with me. The word *truth* points to reality, so a biblical friend brings people out of fantasy and into reality.

4. UNMOVABLE RELIABILITY

One who has unreliable friends soon comes to ruin,
but there is a friend who sticks closer than a brother.

Proverbs 18:24

It is dependability and trustworthiness that make a good friend. It is having faith in a person's ability to hold your weight, and you theirs. *Can I sit on you? When the weight of my life falls, will you move?* If the religious officials tempt you with silver like they did Judas, a true friend will remain unmovable.

Reliability is predictability. We must be careful to discern the reliability of our friends. Fortunately, this is a trait that leaves clues. At times when we are deceived by people who appear reliable but aren't, it may be that we trusted too soon or were in denial. The reliability of a person is often something we soon get clues about if we are paying attention.

5. UNCEASING ENCOURAGEMENT

Two are better than one,
because they have a good return for their labor:
If either of them falls down,
one can help the other up.
But pity anyone who falls
and has no one to help them up.

Ecclesiastes 4:9–10

Think of it like this. Our principles are the map, offering direction for the life road ahead. We are the cars, the vessel moving along the road toward our destinies. So where are our relationships in this metaphor? Well, we can think of the encouragement of our friends as the gas that can keep us going. Friends are who God uses to fill us up. There are some things we will never achieve without the encouragement and influence of our friends.

An authentic friendship not only gives us joy and helps us become who God intended us to become, but this category of relationship also helps us do what we could not do alone. This is true whether this is a friendship with someone you met in college or the friendship within a marriage or family.

I mentioned this briefly a couple of times before, but let's return to the creation story of Adam and Eve. Most people consider the story of the first human relationship in terms of intimacy. Yet there are other principles in the creation narrative that apply across all relationships. Eve enters Adam's life and is called "a helper suitable for him" (Genesis 2:18). Now let's not see "helper" through the traditional Western patriarchal lens. Remember, the Holy Spirit is also called a "Helper" (John 14:16, 26; 15:26; 16:7 ESV). Eve as "helper" is a powerful demonstration of how the ability to move forward with your purpose is often 100 percent contingent on the help that God sends into your life in the form of a friend.

● ● ●

So let's take a moment to reflect once more: Do the people you call friends demonstrate these traits? If not, I would argue it's time to raise your RQ, because if you don't, you just might be setting yourself up for a major relationship breakdown.

THE JOY IN FRIENDSHIP

One of the great benefits of relationships like these is joy. God has created relationships for our enjoyment. Think about it! The greatest gift that God gave humanity was the gift of relationship with him through Jesus. Likewise, people can be such an enjoyable part of our lives. The Scriptures reveal that God says that evidence of his work in the life of a believer will be joy. Yes, it may be elusive at times, even fleeting, as life carries us through ups and downs. But God promises to improve the emotional quality of our life by giving us joy.

Whenever I mention enjoyment as an intention of God, some argue that an emphasis on joy is selfish. But this isn't some self-centered theology. Joy is not a selfish pursuit. We should unashamedly, unapologetically pursue it because God promises it. And one of the ways we get our joy is through relationships. When relationships are functioning according to God's design, we're able to experience this joy without exploiting, abusing, or manipulating the people we are in relationship with.

I've seen people get joy from a number of things. I think we all do. But I'm not sure there is anything that sustains joy like friendships. I've heard of people hugging cars when they get a new one. They say, "Oh, I love my car!" But no one hugs a car the way they hug a person.

As a pastor who has the privilege and blessing of speaking

and being with people, of walking with people through end-of-life situations, I've never heard anyone on their deathbed say, "I want my car." They always ask for people. They ask, "Where's so-and-so? Is so-and-so coming?" Because nothing gives us joy like authentic friendships. This is a very important litmus test for a strong friend: *Do they bring me joy?*

IRON SHARPENERS

Friendships also develop us. Proverbs 27:17 reads, "As iron sharpens iron, so one person sharpens another." Essentially this is equivalent to saying that association produces assimilation. Without a doubt, good friendships help us become what we could not become without those relationships.

Transformation doesn't come just from information. You can read a hundred books on how to become a kinder person. But it's in your relationships that your ability to be kind is refined. Transformation comes from relationships, but more specifically, it comes from exposure to the example you're shown in a relationship. These examples inspire you to do things differently or better. That's how you know you have a solid friendship. You will see yourself grow and become better as a result of interacting with that person.

My friend Terrance, whom I mentioned earlier, had this kind of impact. My exposure to Terrance's emotional quality of life shifted something for me. He seemed happier, more consistent, and clearer in his decision making. He was rarely irritated. His way of moving through the world created an appetite in me to pursue a higher quality of life emotionally and spiritually. He is a great example of this truth: there are some people we can never become until some people come into our lives.

THE POWER OF THE ONE

When I consider my relationship with my college friend Terrance, I think it's a powerful picture of the way relationships should work. Interestingly enough, I'd grown up in church my whole life. I had been doing church regularly. But somehow, in that season of my life, it would take a singular friendship for me to receive a breakthrough. This is the power of *the one*.

Corporate gatherings, conferences, seminars, and workshops are all great. They deliver great information to process and try to apply. But these events are supplements. They work only in conjunction with individual relationships. There is a reciprocal nature to one-on-one engagement that is crucial for the development of friendships and cannot happen in a large auditorium or classroom.

And reciprocity shouldn't be confused with uniformity. We will never be able to give back to someone in a relationship *exactly* what they give to us. But we can give something. Reciprocation is a way to steward relationships.

Reciprocation helps us minimize the likelihood of exploitation in relationships. It prevents us from using people and being used. As we continue to examine the various categories of relationships, we will want to keep in mind the concept of deposit and withdrawals. Where there are more withdrawals than deposits in any friendship, that relationship is going to experience a degree of bankruptcy. At some point, there's going to be exploitation, and that is not good stewardship of our relationships. And sure, the reciprocation may not be in the same denominations. It may not even be to the same degree. But some giving on both sides should be present in order for the relationship to survive.

Jesus gives us an example in Luke 17:11–15:

> Now on his way to Jerusalem, Jesus traveled along the border between Samaria and Galilee. As he was going into a village, ten men who had leprosy met him. They stood at a distance and called out in a loud voice, "Jesus, Master, have pity on us!"
>
> When he saw them, he said, "Go, show yourselves to the priests." And as they went, they were cleansed.
>
> One of them, when he saw he was healed, came back, praising God in a loud voice. He threw himself at Jesus' feet and thanked him—and he was a Samaritan.

In this gospel account, Jesus runs into ten men who had leprosy. He tells them to go show themselves to the priests. As they're going to show themselves to the priests, they get healed. One stops, turns, and comes back to Jesus and says, "Thank you." In the following verses, Jesus asks, "Where are the other nine?" (Luke 19:17).

Now that man could not give to Jesus what Jesus gave to him. Jesus didn't *need* that man with leprosy to give to him what he gave to him. Jesus didn't need healing from leprosy. But the man did give Jesus something. He gave Jesus his thanksgiving. He made a deposit where he got a withdrawal. So sometimes, in some relationships and certainly in strong friendships, reciprocation is appreciation. It's encouragement. Even God expects thanksgiving. We reciprocate not just because the other person needs to receive it but because we need to do it.

NURTURING FRIENDSHIPS

Friends are rare. That may be hard to realize, but it is nonetheless true. Yet, when we have friendships that are functioning the way God intended for them to function, our friends can become supplements to and sometimes substitutes for family. There's no other word used more in the New Testament to describe the church than family. When you consider the language you use in the church, it assumes our community is like a family—household of faith, brothers and sisters, spiritual parents. It's a family because God has ordained it as a space where those of us who may come from natural families where there are deficits and dysfunctions, communities where we didn't get what we need, can have a second family. We don't have to live life imprisoned by the decisions of our first family.

These types of relationships are so valuable that they should be nurtured with appreciation. Sure, that appreciation is going to manifest differently, depending on the person. As author Gary Chapman talks about in his book *The 5 Love Languages*, love in friendships can show up as words of affirmation, quality time spent, gifts given and received, or acts of service.[6] However it appears, appreciation is necessary.

Friendships should also be nurtured and managed (stewarded) with humility. When there is the absence of humility in any relationship dynamic, there is likely the presence of entitlement. The goodness we receive from our friends is not necessarily a gift we deserve. In fact, good friends are a grace gift by virtue of God being the one who orchestrates their presence in our lives.

So it's incredibly important to humbly manage our friendships and invest in them. Time is our most valuable, precious commodity. It is irreplaceable. Once you lose it, it is gone forever. So time should be the currency we invest into the things we care the most about. Friends prioritize each other. They make time to speak and engage with each other. All of that takes an investment of time. When the seed of time is sown, the harvest of intimacy is reaped, and a life is changed.

THE POWER OF CONNECTION

The quality of our lives is greatly determined by who's in them and by how I manage the ones who are a part of them. In other words, the people I allow to occupy space in my life can contribute to my experience of abundant life, or they can contribute to my life being an agitating one.

When we look at the litany of Scriptures on the reality of relationships, we see a picture of possibility being painted—a picture we should all passionately pursue. We see that kingdom relationships have the potential to be fruitful, and not just in the romantic sense as demonstrated, say, in Song of Songs. All our relationships have the potential to be fruitful, flourishing, and fulfilling. In fact, think of fruitful as meaning there is something produced as a result of the relationship that would not be produced if we hadn't come together. Again, sometimes we see this only in the context of marriage or romantic relationships, but it extends so far beyond.

Connection gives us more than company. Connection enables us to produce things, to be productive in ways we would not be if we hadn't come together. It's when an individual is an asset in your life and not just a liability. This is God's intent for us. We can think of it as God's Canaan land for our relationships. The best relationships are the ones where the people involved actually want to be. Where, if one party is away, the other feels like they're operating at some degree of a deficit when they're separated from each other.

The soundness of our relationships, whether or not they're flourishing, sometimes can be determined by whether we are sad when a person leaves but excited when they come back. There's vitality. There's veracity. There's the unexplainable, incommunicable "it" factor. It's the ability to say, "I know you more, and I don't love you less." When engaged in an authentic friendship, deficits are resolved. They are no longer deficits when a person occupies space in our lives. The person we call friend becomes the person God chooses to use to address issues in our lives that weren't addressed before they got there. And we are okay with that. We feel safe.

We shouldn't feel the same way in our friendships that we feel, say, on the job. Friendships are not jobs. On the job we are simply exchanging gifts. If I don't bring my gifts, skills, talents, or abilities to the job, then there would be no relationship. It's transactional. Even as a pastor, I know that my congregation loves me, but it's in many ways a transactional relationship. I use my gifts to serve the body.

But the relationships we have with people we call friends, people we choose to do life with, should be covenantal, not transactional. Those relationships are the one place where we're able to be our authentic selves. We should be able to say, "This is who I am, and this is the one place I don't have to be anyone other than who God made me to be." This doesn't mean we don't grow or evolve. It means that the core of our close and intimate relationships is a kind of acceptance.

As a guide going forward, we should know this: authentic friendship affirms. We shouldn't feel like a politician in our own relationships, where we have to measure every word and spin every conversation. Where we have to tell half-truths because we can't tell the whole truth. Where we're walking on eggshells. Our friendships should be uninhibited in many ways. A place where we are unashamed. Our relationships are full of affection, though not the handsy kind. Bottom line, they are vessels for an enormous manifestation of God's unconditional love for us.

Category #2

ASSOCIATES

The second category of relationships is a category called "associates." This category is frequently confused with category #1—"friends." A person's relational intelligence is what enables them to discern the difference. An associate is a person with whom you have periodic or consistent association. An associate is what I call a "tweener relationship." It is a category that describes a person who is not in the friendship category, but not in the assignment or advising categories either.

A person should be assigned to the associate category when there hasn't been enough time, interest, or desire to develop the kind of connection required for friendship. It's a relationship where a person doesn't prefer to, for whatever reason, engage any deeper than the surface. Maybe there is a lack of chemistry or few mutual interests. Maybe there are character inconsistencies that make you feel unsafe around them.

Jesus often used animal metaphors to describe the personality of people. One of the animals he uses to describe one type of personality is a goat. A goat is a tweener animal. It isn't a sheep, but it isn't a wolf either. Goats are very unpredictable in their behavior. At times they can be docile and calm, and other times they are very aggressive. Likewise, there are people to whom you stay close enough to milk but far enough away from so you don't get bit. Goats also eat garbage. Therefore, you should be authentic around them but not transparent. They don't need to know the more intimate details of your life.

Sometimes associate relationships are the consequence of intersecting schedules. This may include a person who lives nearby or goes to the same school, or it may be a coworker. In fact, it's quite possible that some of us spend more time with a coworker during the week than family and friends. As a result of that proximity and time spent, a degree of relationship will have developed. However, this doesn't mean this person is a friend. It is possible to not spend the most time with the people you care about the most. Even so, it's unwise to have the same expectations of this person that you would of a friend.

A DIFFERENCE IN EXPECTATIONS

One of the different expectations of an associate relationship should be in the area of reciprocity. You shouldn't expect the same type of reciprocity from associates that you do from friends. Associate relationships are generally unbalanced relationships. For example, a person may be willing to share details of their lives with us, but we don't trust them enough yet to share our details with them. We may be willing to let someone borrow money on occasion, but we would never ask them for the same favor. These are lopsided exchanges and often mean that both parties are associates rather than friends. When we understand and embrace this reality, we are able to temper our expectations and consequently minimize our frustrations.

Relational frustration can often be a result of failed expectations. If a person's expectations are constantly not met, then their frustration can mutate into disappointment. Jesus often aligned his followers' expectations with reality so they could govern themselves accordingly. He provides a powerful picture of relational intelligence:

> "Whatever town or village you enter, search there for some worthy person and stay at their house until you leave. As you enter the home, give it your greeting. If the home is deserving, let your peace rest on it; if it is not, let your peace return to you. If anyone will not welcome you or listen to your words, leave that home or town and shake the dust off your feet. Truly I tell you, it will be more bearable for Sodom and Gomorrah on the day of judgment than for that town.
>
> "I am sending you out like sheep among wolves. Therefore, be as shrewd as snakes and as innocent as doves."
>
> *Matthew 10:11–16*

In this passage, Jesus is sending people on ministry assignments. Yet he does not send them out empty-handed. First of all, he gives *power*. Power is ability, authorization, and assistance. Just because a person has the ability doesn't mean they are authorized. Next, Jesus gives them a *plan*, which in today's language is sometimes called "best practices," for carrying out the role. Finally, there is something else that Jesus gives that is just as significant. He gives them *perspective*. He tells them what to expect and informs them on how to handle rejection. Why would Jesus teach people how to respond to rejection if they weren't going to experience it and if it wasn't important to know how to manage it? He aligns their expectations so they aren't surprised by the inevitable. Just as Jesus did this for them, he wants to do it for us. It's important to have expectations aligned so we don't expect associates to behave like friends or don't live with the pressure of being forced to treat associates like friends.

Listen to what Jesus says to the disciples: "I'm sending you out as sheep among wolves." In other words, "You're going to have one disposition, but I'm sending you out among people who are going to have a completely different disposition. You're going to be like a sheep, but they're going to be like wolves—aggressive, assertive, hostile—and you're going to find yourself being bit by people you're just trying to feed." In effect, Jesus is saying, "You're going to find yourself trying to help people, and they're going to be treating you like you're hurting them. You're going to try to engage in ministry and some people are going to misinterpret your motives, and they're going to confuse your trying to advise them with your trying to arrest them."

And most of us would respond with, "I got enough business of my own to get into yours. I don't need anybody else's business. I'm here not because I need to be. I'm here because I want to be. I'm here because I love you and believe in you, and I refuse to let you go without a fight. I refuse to let the adversary have his way with you and not do anything about it. I refuse to sit on the sidelines and let you live less than God's best. That's why I'm in your face. It's because you're on my heart."

But as I mentioned, Jesus gives the disciples and us

perspective so we're not surprised by the inevitable. He says, "I want you to have a realistic perspective about what's about to happen." He teaches them how to respond to people who won't listen. He says, "Before you leave, I want to tell you what to do when people don't listen." He says, "I know you got power, but they are still not going to listen. I know you got a great plan, but some people still are not going to listen. And I know I'm going to tell you what to preach and you're going to say what I told you to say and some people still aren't going to listen." Jesus will say, "I know this to be true because they didn't listen to me."

In particular, friendships have more emotional reciprocity. There is an emotional bond on the part of both parties that doesn't necessarily exist with associates. The nature of our emotional attachment to a friend is different. The way we demonstrate our care is different also. All of this is okay. In fact, it's not only okay, but it's intelligent. You are a limited finite being with limited time and energy. We all must strategically steward it in ways that align with our priorities. This is the key to fruitfulness and fulfillment in life. You will be most fulfilled and most fruitful when your proclaimed values line up with your actual priorities. This applies relationally also and is the reason the investment you make into friends isn't the type you may make in an associate.

A DIFFERENT KIND OF INVESTMENT

The investment between associates is different. With friends, we are willing to sometimes make even sacrificial investments in the relationship. Friendships will cost us time, emotional bandwidth, and sometimes money. This may not be the case with an associate. We are not as likely to make the same kind of sacrificial investments in the relationship, not because we don't value the person, but more because we don't value the relationship to the same degree as we do with our friends.

This is where we often become confused. Those of us who make the mistake of making sacrificial investments in associate relationships are generally those who tend to conform and contort ourselves to other people's preferences—in other words, people-pleasers. We have the disease to please, or we carry misguided guilt and erroneous expectations. We do not have the ability to say no nicely.

This is a problem that Stephen Covey says is incredibly damaging to our relationships. He writes, "You have to decide what your highest priorities are and have the courage—pleasantly, smilingly, nonapologetically—to say no to other things. And the way you do that is by having a bigger *yes* burning inside. The enemy of the best is often the good."[7] Unfortunately, too many of us are concerned way more than we should be about the way we will be perceived. We feel like it's not going to be advantageous for us educationally, professionally, etc. And so we invest in people who don't reciprocate that investment and we wonder where we went wrong.

OF LITTLE CONSEQUENCE, UNTIL . . .

The truth that associate relationships often have little consequence in a person's life is sometimes challenging to hear. But there is hope! A person can be an associate even as we are in a season of discernment, determining if we are safe enough with the person to move them into the category of friend.

We'll talk more in later chapters about the process of discernment that must happen as we consider moving a person from one category to another, but here are a couple of questions we should ask ourselves: *Do I trust them? Do I see character flaws that are good and healthy for me?* It's entirely possible there hasn't been enough time to figure out a person yet, and that over time, it would be possible to have a genuine, organic connection with them.

In every relationship, we're always watching and discerning, but when a person reaches the friendship category, he or she is a person you've probably already gone through the discernment process with and understand their behavior. A friend is generally reliable and dependable, or if they aren't, we know it clearly and the reasons for it. This isn't the case yet with an associate. We are still in the learning phase with them, trying to figure them out. Hence the reason I call it a tweener relationship.

Associates aren't friends. Some will never be. Others may be one day. But in the current relationship, there is no emotional bond and attachment with them. They aren't in the assignment or advisor categories either. Associate relationships are like this: "Yeah, we share a little bit of ourselves with each other. Maybe it's the fact that we don't like peanut butter or we're both out to find the best schools to enroll our children in. But I don't feel any pressure to share any more with you. Maybe you do. Maybe you don't. If you do, I may not have the desire to go there with you. And that's okay."

I'll make calls for friends that I may not make for an

associate. I'll open doors for friends that I may not open for an associate. I'll put my name on the line in a way for friends that I may not do for an associate.

THE DIFFERENCE IN IMPACT

The impact or outcome of an associate relationship is inevitably going to be different. The enjoyment, development, and achievement that I talked about in the previous chapter—markers of a relationship—will be less across the board in associate relationships.

Your relationship with an associate does not impact you the same way your friendships do. And it doesn't have to. It's easy to get confused by that fact. *Because aren't we supposed to love everyone?*

Our lack of discernment in this area is too often a function of spiritual guilt. We've bought the lie that we are supposed to feel the same way about everybody. But biblically this isn't even true. There are several ways to love that show up in the Bible. And the one often talked about—*agape*, a Greek word—actually has nothing to do with feelings at all. It's a love of the will. It's an unconquerable benevolence. It's commitment to do what's in the best interest of someone else, regardless of what they do for you.

So for some of us, it's difficult to discern whether we should be treating someone with *agape* love, which is the godly love we are supposed to offer every human being on the planet, or the *phileo* (brotherly/sisterly) love that is specific to a relationship. This confusion leads to treating associates like friends and getting burned by people who were never safe to begin with.

It's okay if a relationship doesn't impact you emotionally. It's okay if a relationship you have with an associate isn't as consequential to your life and your future. It's just a fact. It's a reality of life. And it doesn't mean you don't love people the way the Scriptures instruct us to love them. It just means that you're honest. You are clear that the nature of your emotional attachment to them is not the same, and so the relationship is not as consequential for you in those areas.

THE THREE, THE TWELVE, AND THE OTHERS

Jesus modeled the tiered nature of relationship for us. Jesus had three disciples who were closest to him—these could be considered friends. He had the remaining disciples, or the Twelve, who would also be considered friends, only with varying degrees of engagement (think our criteria: enjoyment, development, and achievement). And then there are the others, the seventy-plus who traveled with Jesus during his ministry. They might be considered associates. Maybe even some of the Twelve were associates. Nevertheless, Jesus made clear distinctions in his relationships.

DON'T BE FOOLED

I'd like to return to the story of Joab and David in 2 Samuel 18 that I briefly mentioned in the previous chapter. It paints a powerful picture of the roles of friends and associates.

Joab was, first of all, a military leader for a king named David. He was seemingly very loyal to him. When Absalom, David's son, rebelled against the king and attempted a coup, David was left with just his mightiest men, including his friend Joab. This seems like the perfect picture of friendship because friends are loyal even when that loyalty is being tested in the face of other opportunities. In other words, we don't know if a person is loyal until they have the opportunity not to be. Loyalty is revealed in the presence of other opportunities, in the face of inconvenience. Some people are loyal when it's easy to be. Their true loyalty is revealed by their actions in our absence.

With Joab, things weren't as they seemed.

So David gives his instructions. He basically says, "Listen, do not kill my son Absalom." He clearly doesn't want Absalom killed. Unfortunately, Joab goes out and kills Absalom anyway. David is inconsolable. He immediately replaces Joab, but Joab kills the guy David replaces him with.

Later, David and Bathsheba have their son Solomon, who is certain to become the next king. But there is some infighting, and another man—Adonijah—is, for a while, set up to become king (1 Kings 1). And despite how loyal Joab once was to David, he aligns himself with this other king nominee and not Solomon. As you might guess, the relationship between Joab and David is completely dissolved at that point—so much so that when David prepares himself to die, he gives Solomon his parting instructions. He essentially tells Solomon, "If you're going to have a peaceful reign, you're going to have to kill Joab" (see 1 Kings 2:5–6).

Joab, to me, is an example of how associates can show up wearing friend's clothes. They look like friends on the outside, and maybe they do things here and there to demonstrate their friendship, but on the inside, they don't have your best interests at heart. Or their character is diminished by circumstances beyond your control. Joab obviously had some character issues. His motives were suspect, and that reality ultimately revealed itself.

Granted, we all have imperfections. You aren't going to find a friend without flaws. But all imperfections are not created equal. Some imperfections are more consequential in relationships. Joab, for a great amount of time, looked like a friend to David. But in the end, what we saw was that he was actually an associate, because he chose opportunity over the relationship. He was ultimately disloyal. Unhelpful. All to a man he'd served and done life and ministry with for so long.

Here is your clue: anyone who would harm or disregard you for an opportunity is not someone who should be in the friend category. They are associates at best. Associates can be opportunistic (see Judas, the disciple of Jesus). Your awareness of that fact will save you many headaches and heartbreaks.

WHO DO WE TAKE WITH US?

I've seen the "friend versus associate" dynamic play out in my church. For instance, there were two people who served together on a team in our church. Their relationship was the result of intersecting schedules. They didn't know each other. The only way they had come to know each other was through church and through spending time together in the context of the ministry in which they were serving.

One person was going through some challenges in her personal life and felt a degree of comfort with the other person.

The other person obviously did not. The person who was struggling began to share some of her issues because she felt this person who she did ministry with was her friend. She assumed this, despite no real engagement outside of church. Her assumption also included thinking that the person she was sharing her heart with would keep her story confidential—because that's what a friend would do.

Unfortunately, that did not happen. The person shared these challenges with another person in the church—one of her actual friends—and this information spread like wildfire throughout the body. The woman's imperfections were so exposed to such a large group of people—people she believed were her spiritual family—that she chose to move to another part of the country. She learned in the most devastating way that this person with whom she served was not a friend at all. The emotional damage that occurred in the fallout was vast and caused her to distrust most people after that. She took the wrong person "to the garden" with her, and her life was forever changed.

So let's return to the example of Jesus and the three, twelve, and others.

Jesus took Peter, James, and John—his three—to the Mount of Transfiguration (see Matthew 17). He *didn't* take Doubting Thomas. To be clear, that is not a judgment on Thomas. It's more of a statement of the role Thomas played in the group. It also says that certain imperfections can't be trusted in certain places in our lives.

BE KIND: A FINAL STORY

There were two pastors who were very good friends, and both of them were pursuing an opportunity in a church that was looking for a new pastor. Both of them were senior pastors of their own churches but were looking to move on to a better opportunity in a different kind of city. They both applied for the appointment and were aware that the other was applying.

During the process, they had to do some interviewing, and during the interviewing stage, one pastor learned that the other pastor wasn't speaking well about him to the pulpit search committee. As a result, the pastor who did the bad-mouthing won the position, and the other lost a potential opportunity.

But more than the lost opportunity, the pastor who believed his friend wouldn't do such a thing lost faith—yes, in that particular person, but in people generally. He became walled off, and in the words of Henry Cloud and John Townsend, instead of putting up "fences that were strong enough to keep the bad out and gates in those fences to . . . let in the good,"[8] he put up walls that kept everything out, both the good and the bad. He isolated himself significantly because a person he called a friend—who was really an associate—used information that he had shared in confidence to create an advantage for himself. There was a dramatic impact that affected him vocationally, financially, emotionally, and spiritually, all because he took the wrong person to the garden with him.

So one of the key ways a person moves from associate to friend, to being someone who wants to go to the garden, so to speak, is to learn to keep a person's confidences. Be a cup, not a faucet. Receive their heart, but don't spread it. If a person trusts you enough to share some of the things you would only share with a friend, then even as an associate—as a good person, period—keep their story confidential. This could potentially be the beginning of a shift relationally, or it could just be a way to be kind as a person of faith. Either way, there are no losers.

Category #3

ASSIGNMENTS

It's often suggested that one of the church's primary purposes is to be the educational arm of the kingdom of God. In other words, the church has been given the responsibility to be the entity that provides spiritual education and formation to those who have received the life-changing love of God through Jesus Christ. The textbook that the church is to use is the Word of God. Second Timothy 3:16 says that all Scripture is "God-breathed and is useful for teaching, rebuking, correcting and training in righteousness." Rebuking, or reproof, is probably the function most relevant for this book and this chapter because reproof deals with the dismantling and demolishing of wrong perspectives and paradigms. There is a way that we see life, the world, and the people in it that is fundamentally flawed, and the Word of God has to become the wrecking ball that demolishes our ways of thinking that are misguided, misinformed, and destructive.

Based on my personal experience and pastoral observation,

the church has been aggressive and intentional about knocking down the walls and transforming the ways we see certain disciplines. We are taught how to pray, praise, love, serve, and give. However, we seem to have overlooked an area that is equally important yet underemphasized—and that area is relationship management. Consequently, we have raised up a people who can get along with God, but no one else. We relate to each other based on assumptions, culture, family patterns, and personal philosophies, and not the way the most profound relationship guru, Jesus, did. Too often we ignore the reality that we've been taught to do everything except how to do relationships. One of the unfortunate consequences of this reality is that we completely misunderstand the role of the assignment.

The assignment category is an interesting one because it is most commonly misinterpreted or misapplied. An assignment is a trainee, a mentee, an advisee. This type of relationship exists primarily for the purpose of one person providing mentorship, guidance, training, and coaching to another. At the risk of sounding insensitive, assignments are people projects. They are projects that we decide to take on, projects assigned because of our work, or projects given to us by God.

A key quality of the assignment category of relationship is that it is a lopsided exchange. Assignments are people in whom you will make deposits, but from whom you will more than likely not receive withdrawals. This doesn't mean assignments can't or won't make any contribution to our lives. It simply means the nature of the relationship is one that exists specifically for the purpose of you giving to someone what you may have received from someone else.

In truth, the assignment relationship can be parasitic. I very much mean this in a scientific sense as opposed to the negative colloquial way it's used in our culture. A parasite is a biological organism that lives and is sustained at the expense of the host. They release waste and toxins into the body of the host and feed off of the host, offering no adequate or useful return. Parasites show up in the human body in a number of ways, and each of these metaphorically line up with the way the assignment role will function in our lives. These include the following:

1. *Sleep disorders*. In the night, the body works to eliminate toxins via the liver. Parasitic infections can interrupt this process and upset the rhythms of the body. They disrupt sleeping patterns. In an effort to serve our assignments and give them what they need for their journey, we may find our rest disrupted.
2. *Teeth grinding*. This condition occurs most often at night, and it may be linked to the restlessness and anxiety caused in the body by the parasite's release of waste and other toxins. Grinding is also a popular cultural euphemism that suggests hard work. When a person is working hard, they may say, "I'm on my grind." Assignments often require a little extra work. It could be coffee, phone calls, lunch meetings. They all can produce grinding.
3. *Immune system dysfunction*. When you have a parasite living inside you, it will often leech vital nutrients from the body, forcing the immune system to operate with a poor supply of vitamins, minerals, and energy sources. Parasites also stimulate the production of defenders

against foreign substances, leaving the body susceptible to attacks from bacteria, yeast, fungi, viruses, and other foreign invaders. In our relationships, assignments can pull on that which is vital for you to survive. Your emotions, time, and energies are all invested in this person.

I recognize that this may be an interesting—maybe even challenging—description of the assignment relationship. However, we sometimes give a sanitized version of our expectations with mentorships and fail to provide a realistic picture of their possible ramifications. To be clear, assignments are not necessarily leeches, nor is there no mutual benefit in the relationship. But there is a level of exertion and investment that we will make in an assignment that is very different from what we will make in a friend or an associate.

In assignment relationships, there may even be a *spirit* of friendship, despite a person not actually being a friend. People without relational intelligence are unaware of this reality and could make the mistake of treating an assignment like a friend. When this happens, we end up mismanaging expectations, disclosing what should be confidential, and robbing the assignment of the transformative relationship they were sent to us to get. This is why *alignment* is essential. Your relationships have to be defined and aligned properly. Knowing whether someone is a friend, an associate, an assignment, or an advisor will help manage expectations when it comes to the level of enjoyment, development, and achievement expected from any particular relationship.

Assignments are individuals who may appear to have a genuinely deep admiration for you, but in actuality their love and admiration is for your gift and not for you as a person. In other words, an assignment may have sought you out because of something you have accomplished, and it's the gift, talent, or skill that they're actually enamored by. To ignore this reality is to be like an athlete who doesn't realize that the same fans who will cheer when you play well will be the ones who will boo when you play poorly.

At some point, if your contribution to their life is no longer perceived as valuable, they are likely to leave the relationship. If they do, just make sure you haven't given them any dirt to take with them. When this is understood, you're not setting yourself up for disappointment because of unrealistic expectations. This is not cynicism; it's realism. It's like a saying I once heard: to be surprised by the inevitable is to be naive.

A DIFFERENT KIND OF RELATIONSHIP

What's interesting about assignments is they don't always start out that way. As is the case with all these categories, relationships can evolve and people can shift. I've experienced this myself. I had a long-term relationship with a person—someone I'd known probably for a decade. We were, as I would define it, *friends*. We also had some mutual passions. We were into fashion and even more into video games. I spent a significant amount of time around this person. We hung out, confided in each other, and were deeply involved with each other's families.

Over time, however, I began to notice the shift. First, the nature of our conversations started to change. It went from a mutual sharing to me answering numerous questions.

It transitioned from conversations regarding some personal areas of our lives to very specific questions about our professional lives. He wanted to know how to manage certain things that were coming up for him in ministry.

Now, certainly friends will advise each other from time to time. There is such a thing as peer mentorship, which I believe is extremely important. But the difference between peer mentorship in a friendship and in an assignment relationship is that the assignment relationship is formed, or exists, primarily for that purpose alone. I came to realize that my relationship with this person was evolving from one of friendship to one of assignment, where I was adding value to him in an entirely new and different way than I did as just his friend.

My role had changed in this relationship, and I had to come to terms with that. Our conversations shifted to me primarily advising this person, and as a result, the nature of our bond shifted. The attachment was different than before. I did not love him any less. I did love him *differently* because I didn't feel as emotionally attached to him as I had before.

It's incredibly important to realize that these categories can often be *stages* as opposed to states. They are not always static, but fluid. We must be able to discern and recognize when something is shifting.

Another sign that this relationship was moving from friendship to assignment was my increased awareness that my experience, exposure, and good fortune had become a way for me to add value to his life in a different kind of way. Yes, friends help friends, but this was something different. I had an overwhelming desire and ability to add value to him. It wasn't me doing a friend a solid. It was me strategically placing myself in a position to pour into him and his ministry, with very little emotional investment in the outcomes.

As a result of the change in our conversations, the shift in my input, and the detachment of our intertwined personal lives, I recognized that this man I'd once called a friend had become an assignment. There was a different kind of attachment—less emotional, less intimate, and more focused on helping him grow and succeed.

TRAITS OF AN ASSIGNMENT

So what exactly does an assignment look like? How does an assignment show up? First, an assignment must be someone who sees you as an essential asset. The mentee must really see the mentor as a mentor. The advisee has to see the advisor as someone worthy of seeking advice from. The spiritual son or daughter must view the spiritual father or mother as actual spiritual parents. You cannot help anyone who does not want help from you, and you're never going to be assigned to anyone who doesn't want that help.

Again, there is an awesome example in Matthew 10. Jesus sent his disciples out two by two to various villages. This, I believe, denotes relationships of purpose. The purpose of the disciples' engaging in relationship with one another and with the people they encountered is to add value to the lives they came into contact with, including their own. In the case of an assignment, there may be some mutual exchange but that exchange is likely to have some inequity. And that's got to be okay for you and your assignment. An assignment is not going to pour back into you the way you pour into them. They aren't going to bless you the way that you bless them. That's the whole point!

I'm not just talking about blessing you differently though. It's not just about them pouring into you in a different way, as we sometimes see in friendships. I'm talking about the measure of it. You will probably pour out *more* to your assignment than you'll ever get back from them. So the disciples were certainly going to get some gratitude or maybe a meal from the people in the villages where they are sharing. But what they were giving the people in those villages was so much greater in terms of time and physical and spiritual exertion. The relationship between the disciples and the people assigned to them existed primarily for the purpose of one party adding value to the other. That's the way assignment relationships are structured.

SHAKE THE DUST OFF

When Jesus sends the disciples out two by two, he tells them how to handle the relationships they will encounter along the way. He tells them what to do if the people they meet—the ones assigned to them—don't receive their value well. In effect, Jesus said, "If they don't receive you, shake the dust off your feet, and go to the next city" (see Matthew 10:14).

The disciples are finishing their theological residency. They have been working with Jesus and learning from him, and he huddles with them and prepares them for some field education. He's getting ready to send them out into certain villages and towns to do ministry.

The "shaking the dust off" is a symbol of not taking the residue of rejection from one season or relationship into another. To do so is dangerous. It's also toxic and unhelpful. Many times, your discernment regarding who is or isn't your assignment is going to come through pure experimentation. As you engage in these relationships, more and more will be revealed. You will see an openness in an individual, or a lack thereof. This doesn't mean a person who is potentially your assignment can't eventually open up to you. That's entirely possible. What it does mean is you can't help them until they do.

The truth is, everybody who needs help does not want it from you. As I noted earlier, the person whom God has called to be your assignment is going to be a person who sees you as an essential asset in their life, and as a result, they'll seek you out for advice, coaching, mentorship, and counsel. If they are unwilling to see you in that capacity, make like the disciples and shake the dust off.

Not only must your assignment view you as someone who can help them, but you must see *them* as someone you can help. There will be a sense deep down that you are supposed to help a person. An urge or intuitive push to extend yourself and your resources in their direction. Pay careful attention to this. Every person isn't your responsibility. Every person with a need isn't your assignment. So recognizing the call—the urge to help someone—is an important indication that God is involved.

Acts 16 contains a similar account to the one of Jesus sending the disciples into the villages. Here Paul and his companions are also traveling in different regions. Paul and company had been trying to take the gospel to a number of places. They had attempted to go into Asia and preach there but the Holy Spirit wouldn't allow them to. Then they tried to go to Bithynia, and the Holy Spirit wouldn't allow them to go there either. So they went down to Troas, and during the night, Paul had a vision. A man from Macedonia stood before him and begged, "Come over to Macedonia and help us" (16:9).

When Paul saw the vision, he concluded that God was calling them to preach the gospel in Macedonia. Now here's the thing. Every other place he contemplated going to was certainly a place that needed the gospel. Yet the need of those other places wasn't Paul's responsibility in that moment and season. Paul went where he was called.

So it's one thing for a person to want you to help them; it's another thing to feel God's call, God's push, an intuitive urge that you're supposed to help them.

READY TO HEAR

An assignment is going to be an individual who is open to and ready for the value you're going to add. Pay very close attention to the readiness of the people you feel led to help. An assignment will be someone who not only wants help from you but is open to you giving it the way it needs to be given. If a person is not receptive, the only thing to do is to get out of God's way.

Have you ever tried to feed a baby and the baby tried to help you feed them? Both my kids did that. I would think, *If you would just get out of my way, I could help you.* Well, what if I told you that sometimes our hands can get in the way of what God is doing in our assignments' lives. And God is like, "I kept you when you needed me. I can keep them too. Yes, I've given them to you to pour into, but I didn't give them to you to enable." God is saying, "You may be getting in the way of lessons I want them to learn." God is saying, "You may be ruining a relationship because you're trying to control it, and what's going to happen is that your control is going to breed resentment."

So here is an important point to remember: there are some people we are not able to help. It is crucial to recognize that there are times when we have to walk away from someone who is not quite ready to receive our advisement.

We must discern when people aren't open to being our assignments, even if we believe we've been called to them. In fact, I submit that there are five types of individuals we'll need to surrender to God and pray that he either sends them back to us or to somebody else who is able to help them.

First, *we can't help people who don't think they need it*. Salvation requires that a person acknowledge their need for a Savior (and we are *definitely* not that). We cannot convince someone to take medicine who does not believe they are sick. We cannot convince someone to wear a cast who does not believe their bones are broken. We cannot open people's eyes.

What did Paul do when he dealt with people he felt called to help whose eyes were not open? He prayed for them. That's Ephesians 1. He prayed that the eyes of their heart would be enlightened. When you have a person who doesn't know they need help, we must pray that God will heal them from their blindness before we invest any more time in them as our assignment. If we don't take this approach and keep pressing a person to do things—even good, life-giving things—our conversations are going to start feeling like condemnation.

Second, *we can't help people who know they need it and don't want it*. In John 5, Jesus approaches a man who has had an undisclosed issue for thirty-eight years and asks him this question: "Do you want to get well?" (5:6). See, everything that is bad doesn't feel that way. Some people simply don't want our advisement. They're saying, "I know I should listen. I know this person is pouring their time and resources into helping me reach my full potential. But I just can't. This [insert any distraction] is probably going to kill me, but it's all right. I know I shouldn't be jumping from this to that and this to that, but it's all right." (Of course, we know it's not all right, but there's nothing we can do about that.)

This is especially true when a person becomes a purposeless person. The Bible says, "Where there is no revelation, people cast off restraint" (Proverbs 29:18). We may have an assignment who just doesn't care. They live recklessly because there is no revelation, no vision, for their life. And so they know that even though they may need it, they get to the point where they operate their life carelessly.

Third, *we also can't help people who don't want it yet*. Some people know they want guidance eventually, but they just don't want it *yet*. In my work, these are people who say, "I'm coming to church. I know I need to be there. Just not yet." Or we may hear, "I'm going to stop. I'm going to put it down. I know I need to put it down, but not yet." Or "I'm not going to marry him. We're just kicking it. We're going to break up because he isn't marriage material. But I'm not through with him just yet."

Fourth, *we also can't help people who don't want it from you*. Jesus dealt with this when he went to his hometown in Nazareth.

Jesus returned to Galilee in the power of the Spirit, and news about him spread through the whole countryside. He was teaching in their synagogues, and everyone praised him.

He went to Nazareth, where he had been brought up, and on the Sabbath day he went into the synagogue, as was his custom. He stood up to read, and the scroll of the prophet Isaiah was handed to him. Unrolling it, he found the place where it is written:

> "The Spirit of the Lord is on me,
>   because he has anointed me
>   to proclaim good news to the poor.
> He has sent me to proclaim freedom for the prisoners
>   and recovery of sight for the blind,
>   to set the oppressed free,
>   to proclaim the year of the Lord's favor."

Then he rolled up the scroll, gave it back to the attendant and sat down. The eyes of everyone in the synagogue were fastened on him. He began by saying to them, "Today this scripture is fulfilled in your hearing."

All spoke well of him and were amazed at the gracious words that came from his lips. "Isn't this Joseph's son?" they asked.

Jesus said to them, "Surely you will quote this proverb to me: 'Physician, heal yourself!' And you will tell me, 'Do here in your hometown what we have heard that you did in Capernaum.'"

"Truly I tell you," he continued, "no prophet is accepted in his hometown. I assure you that there were many widows in Israel in Elijah's time, when the sky was shut for three and a half years and there was a severe famine throughout the land. Yet Elijah was not sent to any of them, but to a widow in Zarephath in the region of Sidon. And there were many in Israel with leprosy in the time of Elisha the prophet, yet not one of them was cleansed—only Naaman the Syrian."

All the people in the synagogue were furious when they heard this. They got up, drove him out of the town, and took him to the brow of the hill on which the town was built, in order to throw him off the cliff. But he walked right through the crowd and went on his way.

Luke 4:14–30

Jesus was preaching, and people were like, "Isn't this the carpenter's son? Isn't this Joseph's boy?" Some people's familiarity with Jesus caused them to miss the favor. As advisors, we'll find ourselves in situations where we've been telling an assignment something forever, and then all of a sudden, they call us and start telling us something somebody else said, like it's news. Meanwhile, we're sitting there like, "Wait, fam. Hold up. I've been telling you this for years. I said it better than *they* said it." The key to managing this when this happens is to not take it personally.

Finally, *we can't help people who aren't willing to do what it takes to get what they need.* One time the disciples were challenged by the temple tax collectors over whether Jesus paid the temple tax. Jesus basically told Peter, "You have a provision problem, so I want you to use your gift. Go fishing." Peter went fishing, and when he caught a fish, the coin to pay the temple tax was in its mouth (see Matthew 17:24–27). Sometimes people want coins, but they want you to do the fishing. When that happens, we aren't helping them. We are enabling.

So many of us are dealing with these types of people right now—people who would be assignments but who have resisted our guidance for any number of reasons I've outlined. We may be dealing with parents we're trying to help. Some of us are dealing with substance abuse issues in the family, and we're praying and believing, and they're stealing and leaving. It's hard to give these people up. It's hard when people are not taking your advice but expect you to be there when they're reaping the consequences of not submitting to your counsel.

But God is saying to us, "Do you trust me enough to give them up? Not give up on them, but give them to me and say, 'Lord, the way I've been doing this isn't working, and I want to try it your way.'" God is speaking to us, saying, "Give them to me. Give them up because they're better off in my hands than in yours."

It is sobering though. It can be disconcerting when we are rejected by those we are trying to help. It can produce feelings of rejection because it means we may find ourselves in seasons and situations when we have to sit on the sidelines silently and watch people we care for suffer. We will watch people who have the ability to live better but who are living lives that are beneath their potential. That's truly a different kind of discouragement. And if we don't handle that rejection properly, we will take that rejection personally. And when we take it personally, their rejection can produce an infection called bitterness.

We must embrace the reality of our limitations and accept that some people are just not open. And when you try to force open their engagement, we move out of ministry into manipulation. We move out of calling and into control. There's a word the Old Testament uses to describe people who are obsessively controlling, forceful, and manipulative, even with good intentions—the word is *witchcraft*.

In the Bible, witchcraft is not an old lady with a black hat and a broom stirring broth. It's biblical characters like Jezebel who try to manipulate outcomes so that things turn out the way they think they should turn out. As I've said, Jesus is not encouraging us to give up on people or to stop helping our assignments. What he's doing is trying to rescue us from allowing the rejection that may come to make us so bitter that we resist sowing into people in the future.

ELIJAH AND ELISHA

The Bible offers a really good example of an assignment relationship that demonstrates what the role entails.

To be clear, assignment relationships can still be friendly. There is absolutely an element of friendship in these relationships. When Jesus says to the disciples in John 15:15, "I no longer call you servants . . . Instead, I have called you friends," he is speaking to a relationship that has evolved into multiple dimensions. That said, Jesus' relationships with the disciples was not meant for them simply to keep him company. It was not friendship as we're examining it in this book. He didn't create and cultivate those relationships because he needed confidants. We can think of it like this: Jesus assigned them to himself. He added value to them for the purpose of them adding value to others.

This is important to keep in mind as we examine the relationship between Elijah and Elisha. The relationship between the two existed, not exclusively, but *primarily* for the purpose of Elijah adding value to Elisha. Elisha was assigned to him by God to receive training and equipping. Elijah even lent Elisha the credibility of his name. Elisha was identified in Scripture as the one who "set out to follow Elijah and became his servant" (1 Kings 19:21).

The impartation to this assignment was evident and a great model of what happens at the end of an assignment/advisor relationship. Second Kings 2:15 demonstrates this clearly: "The company of the prophets from Jericho, who were watching, said, 'The spirit of Elijah is resting on Elisha.' And they went to meet him and bowed to the ground before him."

A BALANCED ENGAGEMENT

We should engage with assignments in ways that are much different from the way we engage people we consider friends, associates, or advisors. First, it's critical to have *realistic expectations*. We must own the reality of the nature of our relationship. It can be way too easy to mismanage our relationships with assignments because we have deficits in our relationships with people in other categories. Making an assignment our best friend because our friendships are problematic is a recipe for epic failure and disappointment. It is not realistic, and what will eventually occur is an unintentional and unconscious expectation for a degree of reciprocation that cannot and should not happen. This will ultimately lead to frustration, which can impact what we are supposed to be accomplishing with the assignment.

It's also important to have a *balanced perspective when it comes to authenticity and transparency* in an assignment relationship. One of my mentors once said, "Be authentic with everyone, but transparent with only a few." I carry with me this excellent advice to this day. When it comes to disclosing certain current struggles or fears, it's probably best to share these with a trusted friend or an advisor, not necessarily with someone who is looking to you for guidance. Testimonies and healed places in our lives are great tools for teaching but issues we are currently wrestling through are best shared with an advisor. Remember, the purpose of the assignment relationship is not to be a help to ourselves or to turn our assignment into a confidant; it's solely to add value to the person for their own growth.

So in the assignment relationship, there must be sober expectations and a balance between authenticity and transparency. In addition, there must be *healthy boundaries*—especially in the area of time. The time I spend with an assignment is going to be the time necessary to accomplish whatever my agenda is. As noted earlier, the time investment is different in friendships. With assignments, the investment of time is more purposeful and pointed.

There will also probably be some boundaries we will want to set up in terms of the kind of content that will be discussed and disclosed with an assignment. For example, there are things a person may want to share within the context of an assignment relationship that are better suited to be shared with someone else—especially if it is not an area where we're going to be offering guidance and advice. For example, it's probably not a good idea for a career coach to allow a client to discuss their dating life with them. That could be a violation of a content boundary.

SPACE FOR EVOLUTION

As I alluded to earlier, there must always be space for evolution. These categories can certainly be stages, not states. An assignment relationship can absolutely evolve into a friendship. This generally happens, however, when the nature of the contribution that you've made to the assignment has helped them, matured them, assisted them, or advanced them to the degree that they're able to contribute and reciprocate in a way that a friend might. In other words, the transition from assignment to friend may occur when the assignment doesn't need you in the same way they needed you before.

It's important to note that it is hard to have an authentic friendship with someone who *must* have you as a part of their life in a way that is mostly advisory. One of the qualities of a great friendship is honesty. When a relationship has been in the assignment/advisor stage for a length of time and there is a need for a person's service in one's life, it can affect both parties' ability or willingness to speak the truth in love when there's an attempt to transition to a friendship.

Because of this, it's critical to get to a point in the relationship where we feel like a person has the character to withstand the transition to friendship and we have evidence of a connection to the extent that we feel comfortable managing them the way we would a friend. If you've made the kind of contribution to an assignment's life where you've made them rich when they were poor and added value where there were deficits—but they no longer need those things from you—that's when a transition could be considered. Of course, it's not that they won't ever need your advice again, but it means they have grown and advanced to the place where those needs no longer form the basis of your entire relationship.

On that same point, if your assignment has grown and advanced to a place where those needs are no longer the basis of the relationship but there is no connection or comfort, it's entirely possible that the person will transition from assignment to associate rather than friend.

Category #4
ADVISORS

In certain seasons of our lives, God will bring us advisors. We are their assignments! These individuals will serve as mentors and offer us guidance in specific areas of our lives, usually for a limited amount of time. We may have professional advisors in our career fields. We also may have spiritual advisors whom we allow to pour into us insight, wisdom, and direction. It's crucial that we recognize the advisors God has sent to us and not confuse them with other relationship categories.

ABOVE AND BEYOND

Her name was Darby Ray, and she was more than a professor. When I was deciding whether to abandon my plans to pursue law school and go to seminary, including trying to figure out which seminary to attend, she became my advisor—and ours became one of the most significant relationships I had at the time.

One of the main things I remember about her was that she went above and beyond for me. She did so much more than make sure I got information in the classroom. She guided and counseled me outside of it. She provided me very specific advice when it came to switching gears and majors. I'd worked my whole life to go to law school. I knew I'd be an excellent attorney, and I was excited about the opportunity to provide the kind of quality of life for my family that my parents weren't able to provide for me. That goal was not only important to me, but also to my father.

Dad talked to me quite a bit about making sure I worked hard to put myself in a position to take care of my family. Yet Professor Ray helped me unpack that as my primary reason for wanting to go to law school. It wasn't about a passion for the law. I was trying to counter a narrative I'd seen all my life. She assisted me in evaluating the real factors that were guiding my decisions. She challenged me with questions like, Are you letting your fear of poverty guide your decision? Is this what you want to spend the rest of your life doing?

In one of our conversations, she posed a few additional key questions that helped me lean into the decision to go to seminary. Her guidance, along with encouragement from my then girlfriend, now wife, was one of the primary drivers in deciding which seminary to attend. In fact, she would not do a recommendation for me unless I applied to three schools. In my mind, I had one school that I thought was the ideal place to study. One. It was Professor Ray who widened my vision a bit. I'll never forget her simple question: *What do you envision yourself doing?*

I didn't see myself as simply being relegated to the role of a pastor. I knew deep down I wanted to add value to people's lives outside the context of the church. Professor Ray had actually been demonstrating one of the roles I wanted to take on—that of professor. When I shared that with her, she said something that I'll never forget. "Dharius, it is much easier to start broad and go narrow than it is to start narrow and go broad."

It was almost as if she was saying what Stephen Covey mentions in his book *The Seven Habits of Highly Effective People*: begin with the end in mind.[9] She was challenging me to consider my seminary decision through the lens of ultimately what I wanted to do. I had an important decision to make, one that would attach a degree to me forever. One that would include a school I would have on my résumé for the rest of my life. Professor Ray helped me realize I needed to choose a school that was going to best equip me to do all the things I wanted to do, not just one of the things I felt like I needed to do. I needed a school that would equip me well for the local church, but also for the things I ultimately wanted to do down the road. Beginning with the end in mind was essential.

Even now as I write this book, I serve as an adjunct professor at Princeton Theological Seminary in Princeton, New Jersey. That wouldn't have been possible had it not been for the advice of Dr. Darby Ray. She was a true and trusted advisor in every sense.

THE GUIDANCE OF AN ADVISOR

Having an advisor means that an assignment is able to receive the benefit of someone's experiences, education, and exposure without paying the price the advisor had to pay to get it. It also means that an assignment is the beneficiary of not just the price but the pain paid by that person. Assignments get the lessons without the pain. They get the wisdom without the weeping. They get the perspective without the problems. And an advisor must be willing to accept the lopsided reciprocity this entails.

Covering is a term often used in religious circles. An advisor provides covering. Proverbs 11:14 (ESV) says that in "an abundance of counselors there is safety." So when I say *covering*, it's important to know what type. Consider the difference between a lid and an umbrella. An advisor should never be a lid. A lid covers, yes, but it also limits and contains. An advisor should never limit or contain an assignment. An advisor is more like an umbrella. It covers, but it also keeps us from being exposed to things unnecessarily. Umbrellas quite literally take the hit so we don't have to. Whether we are sitting down or standing up, an umbrella covers us. We can soar like Mary Poppins, and the umbrella will cover us. That's what advisors do.

Advisors definitely keep us from being unnecessarily exposed to certain elements—pain, mistakes, and the like—but they also are catalysts. Our advisors cause things to happen for us that would not happen without them. They help us get further faster. There are lessons and insights they can offer that keep us from experiencing things we don't need to experience.

Finally, advisors are comforters. One of the most incredible things I've experienced from the advisors and mentors in my life is their help in normalizing things that would otherwise feel abnormal. We often don't view our discomfort in a positive light, but many times, that's exactly what we must do—see our temporary discomfort as something that can lead to wonderful change. Our advisors help us do that.

Leaders in local churches can have experiences that easily make them wonder, *What is going on? Why are people doing this? Why do people not show up in the summer?* The advisors in my life have often comforted me in these scenarios by normalizing my experience because they've already gone through what I'm going through. It's a beautiful thing to look at someone who is great and accomplished and know that they've had similar experiences. It's a true comfort.

To be clear, having an advisor is not about pain avoidance. Pain is an unavoidable element of life, and it's often just a part of the way we grow. Yet life is going to give you enough pain, so there's no need to create your own if you don't have to. If some painful experiences can be avoided by receiving advice from someone who's already walked through it, then that's an act of love. That is God loving me through someone else he has chosen to use to help me avoid something that can be damaging to me.

Pain and painful experiences are too often underestimated. We take too lightly the emotional trauma associated with them. As a pastor, I've too often seen people celebrate their survival and their overcoming of painful experiences while being completely unaware of how those experiences have impacted them in ways they need to address and be healed from.

We shout, "I made it through! I survived!" which is great—we absolutely should rejoice. But we don't often look at the ways in which surviving may have made us more cynical or pessimistic or distrusting. We don't examine the residue left behind by our emotional trauma. So if a good advisor can help us avoid some of those traumas, the implications are enormous. What huge added value to our mental and emotional health!

DON'T CREATE CASUALTIES

When you have a family, you are no longer the only one impacted by your decisions. My decisions don't just affect me, they affect my wife, our children, and the spiritual family God has given me. When you're in a company, on a sports team, in a church, your decisions don't affect just you. Other people, people we love, can become casualties of the decisions we make. They can either be burdened by our decisions or blessed by them.

In this regard, advisors are incredibly important because not only do they serve and benefit us in our own lives personally, but they also can help us in terms of the impact our decisions have on others. God uses advisors to protect not just us, but our families as well. Our advisors often are answers to prayers.

ADVICE IS NOT ADVISING

The advisor role can often be confused with other relationship categories. One of the primary ways this happens is when we confuse advisors with people who give advice.

There's a difference.

Just because someone has given us advice doesn't mean they are an advisor. There may be someone—a friend or associate—who has something to offer us in the context of one conversation, but they are not necessarily a person who can consistently play that role in our lives.

This happens often with the associate relationship. An associate hasn't quite demonstrated the characteristics that would classify them as a friend. Yet at the same time, there may be some value they add to your life because they are part of it. That value can be construed as the qualities of an advisor if we aren't careful.

I think from time to time, in these sporadic interactions we have with people, we can assume that the person offering the tidbits of wisdom is an advisor. The challenge is this person may not have a well of wisdom deep enough for us to draw from for the long term. It's the difference between someone adding value for a moment and someone adding value over time and with great significance.

I cannot overestimate the impact of bad advice. It's catastrophic. I see this often in church contexts where people who mean well, whose intentions are pure, and whose hearts are sincere are dishing out advice that's not rooted in the level of exposure and education a person needs. And when I say education, I don't mean college. I just mean training. Their learning has not been robust enough to actually offer people the kind of advice they need to make good decisions. In these cases, Scripture is often twisted or misinterpreted.

For example, instead of teaching discipline and self-restraint, a person pretending to be an advisor may push a couple into a relationship they are not emotionally, financially, spiritually, or psychologically ready to handle. What ensues is calamity and catastrophe—two people hurting each other. Properly identifying who to talk to about what and knowing their level of experience and expertise will go a long way toward helping you identify an advisor and flourish under their counsel.

There are advantages to being able to identify every category of relationship in our lives, and in the next section, we'll do a deep dive into understanding what those benefits are and how they serve us and the people in our lives.

PART 2

Discerning Your Relationships

Once relational categories have been clearly defined, the next step requires us to *learn to discern* who is in our lives, what category they currently occupy, and whether they should actually be there. Without this intentional exercise of discernment, we will live in a constant state of relational murkiness and frustration.

If we are frequently frustrated in our relationships, we must learn to see frustration as our friend. Frustration is an indication that some adjustments need to be made. Frustration is the equivalent of a "check engine" light on our car. It is an indication that the quality of the vehicle we are in is no longer fulfilling.

Frustration is also a result of failed expectations. Therefore, the answer to frustration is often adjusting our expectations. In the context of relationships, it means we must discern whether we are expecting someone to give what they are incapable of or unwilling to give. Some people are not able, and others are not willing. We will stay in frustration when we continually expect someone who belongs in a certain relational category to behave like they belong in another.

REFLECTION

Reflection is an essential aspect of relational intelligence. All of us must be willing to press pause when necessary in relationships. This pausing for reflection enables us to do more than simply be in our relationships; it allows us to also think about them. Relationships are just like any other part of life. It's possible to work *in* one so long that we don't necessarily work *on* it. We can't afford to operate on autopilot with our relational life. We must pause for reflecting, so we can be honest and transparent about what we are feeling, thinking, and seeing in our relationships. The awareness to pause and reflect not only demonstrates EQ (emotional intelligence), but it's the essence of RQ (relational intelligence). Reflection is the starting place.

The first and the most important person we should talk to is ourselves. *Talk to ourselves, Dr. Daniels?* Absolutely. Reflection begins with giving ourselves permission to have a nonjudgmental internal conversation. This is especially true for people of faith. There are times when we are so busy filtering through the appropriateness of what we feel and whether or not it's right to feel it that we don't listen to what our feelings are trying to tell us. In other words, we can easily find ourselves so busy judging our emotions that we don't actually listen to them. I've personally adopted the following axiom for my life: *What I feel is real, even if it isn't right.* I've made a decision to pay attention to how I feel, admit what I feel, and own how I feel before I judge what I feel.

In their book *The Cry of the Soul*, Dan Allender and Tremper Longman suggest that our emotions are messengers. They describe feelings as soldiers on the front line of a battle that are responsible for returning to camp and alerting headquarters to what is going on in the battlefield. "Emotions are not amoral," they write. "They vocalize the inner working of our souls."[10]

Our emotions are God's way of alerting us to something we need to pay attention to. They can alert us to what is going on in our hearts, lives, and relationships. Although they may be unpredictable and difficult to describe, they are still God's gift to us, and they are the language of our heart. Therefore, instead of ignoring them, let's ask ourselves, *What is my heart trying to tell me?*

Engaging in this kind of reflection is so important. We must ask ourselves probing questions: *Am I frustrated? Where? Why? What am I actually expecting that isn't being met? Do I feel bankrupt? Do I feel drained? What am I feeling? Why am I feeling it? What's missing in my life that's needed?* Through reflection, we learn to discern and begin to set things right. To move forward, we start on the *inside* and work our way out.

EVALUATION IS THE KEY

Reflecting on our relationships is crucial because we cannot improve what we don't evaluate. And in truth, that's not just a relationship principle or axiom; it's a reality for almost every area of life. If a person wants to improve their health condition, they have to evaluate it. If a person wants to improve their financial condition, they have to evaluate it. If a person wants to assess how far away they are or how close they are to reaching any goal, there has to be evaluation. So how much more important is it to evaluate how we're feeling about the people in our lives?

Relationships are so consequential to the course, direction, and quality of our lives. I think when things become clearer in our own minds about the roles that people play, decisions become easier. But even before evaluation, we must make space in our minds to reflect and think.

When it comes to the area of relationships, some of these decisions are a bit more cumbersome and complex than these other examples I just mentioned. In the case of a health condition, very often, especially in certain areas, it's black and white. The numbers are either too high or too low. This needs to come down, or this needs to go up. Weight needs to be put on, or weight needs to be taken off. But when it comes to relationships, the emotional attachments we have to people can often be intoxicating to the degree that they impair judgment. Intoxication is not just limited to alcohol. We can be intoxicated by emotions. It's not an evil thing—just a reality that must be considered when it comes to decision making within relationships.

There are times when we've had such a long history with people—people who have made drastic contributions to our lives—that it's difficult to see the relationship as it currently exists. There are also times when we fear the unknown and the uncertain and the discomfort that comes with exploring new relationships with new people. We will hold on to the old because we're comfortable. But if a person doesn't take the time to create the space to ask some key and critical questions of themselves about the people in their lives, they won't have the clarity they need to do the aligning that needs to be done. This is true across all relationship dynamics. It applies to a marriage, and it applies to business. It's possible to be so engaged in being married that you never work on the marriage. It's entirely possible to be so preoccupied with working *in* the business that you never work *on* the business.

And so assessment in any area is the key to advancement. Reflection helps us to act not just emotionally, but intelligently. Relationship alignment is all about decisions, and relational intelligence is all about the relationship decisions we make. Decisions are like cars, and every decision has a driver. Where you end up is determined by who's behind the wheel. Reflection helps us pause for a moment and access the information we need to see who and what is driving. If not, we will end up making blind and bad decisions when it comes to relationships. Many relationships crash because they have no clue who is behind the wheel. It's incredibly hard to make good decisions with bad information.

Taking a moment to pause allows us to emotionally sober up and allow principle, good judgment, and God's Spirit to be the drivers of the decisions we make when it comes to our relationships.

A LACK OF ATTENTION

When we don't take a moment to evaluate what we're feeling and what is happening in a relationship, we end up operating in the dark. It's the same thing that happens when we don't take a moment to evaluate what we're feeling in our body. The same thing that can happen when we don't take time to evaluate what's happening in our emotional life. If we find ourselves spinning out of control, heading in a downward trajectory, going to deep, dark places, it's probably because we have not stilled ourselves to think about what is happening. When a person is unwilling or unable to adequately assess the path and the direction they're going, they're going to end up crashing at some point. Most of all, when we don't take a moment to evaluate our relationships, we assume they belong in a category of our life that they don't and end up damaging them, us, or often both.

THE COURAGE TO PRESS PAUSE

You may be asking, "How do we press pause and reflect appropriately? What exactly should one do in order to correct any misalignments?" *Have the right perspective.* Perspective is more important than the practice or method you choose. The way we see the function of relationships in our lives is much more important than what we do. We certainly should be considerate of how some of our choices to press pause or realign people make others feel, yet our choices cannot be driven by, dominated by, or greatly influenced by others' feelings. In other words, some choices we will make may offend people. But that doesn't mean we're being offensive.

We are solely responsible for the stewardship of our own lives, and we cannot be held hostage by the feelings or expectations of others. Again, this doesn't mean we are cold or inconsiderate. It doesn't mean we don't approach these decisions with compassion. What it does mean is that there are a number of other factors that impact the way people feel about and interpret what we do. Their emotional state creates and produces a filter that impacts how they hear what we say and how they interpret what we do. Understanding this isn't easy, even if it makes things clearer. It certainly requires courage.

Relational intelligence isn't just about clarity; it's also about courage. It's about summoning up the courage to make the decisions that are in the best interest of the life God wants us to steward. And it is believing that my purpose never comes at the expense of someone else's, that the quality of my life never comes at the expense of someone else's if I'm doing it God's way.

A DIFFERENT PAUSE FOR EVERY SEASON

Pressing pause and taking a moment to reflect is going to look different, depending on your season of life. There are times, practically speaking, when pressing pause relationally won't require you to make an announcement that you're pressing pause. There are times when a change in your life will necessitate a change in the relationship, and the change in your life actually gives you the space to do some reflecting. For example, maybe you have a new baby, which requires way more attention at home, so the nature of a particular relationship is going to shift to the point where you can reasonably do some reflecting that you didn't have to announce.

Practically, we can press pause in a couple of ways. First, we can reflect on our relationships when things in life happen that necessitate space for us to do so. It could be a new job, vacation, sabbatical, family issues, promotion, and the like. Those scenarios provide a cover, if you will.

Second, there will be times when the nature of the decision you have to make requires that you take a little bit more time—time that's noticeable and may require a conversation. In those moments, we have to communicate significantly to those who are going to be most affected by our distance.

We'll talk more about that in a later chapter, but when we are in relationships that require some time to process and we don't take the time to do so, the other person may fill in the blanks with their own reasons. This can cause pain and problems, and so it's best to err on the side of communicating openly and honestly.

A decision we have to make for our lives shouldn't come off as an accusation or attack against the character of somebody else. When we're having those conversations, we should essentially say, "Listen, there are a number of different shifts that are taking place in my life, and right now I just need some time to do some reflecting on what I need to do to be a good steward of our relationship and what God is doing in this season. I'm going to need a little while to think through that." Notice that the focus is on the speaker's life. It's not speaking to any specific character flaw in the other person or disparaging their part in the relationship. This is not the place for accusations.

Think of this as an opportunity to communicate what *you* need in your life, and why *you* are taking ownership of this decision.

LEARNING FROM JAMES AND TOM

I recently had an experience where a gentleman I was mentoring—I'll call him James—called me while I was driving. When I answered the phone, he sounded emotionally bothered and confused, since he was dealing with a complex situation.

He said, "There's something I want to talk to you about."

"Okay," I said.

James mentioned that there was something he was experiencing with one of his best friends—I'll call him Tom. James and Tom were close. They got together weekly to hang out. Their families were super close, and they were both in the same line of work. Unfortunately, he'd begun to feel like the nature of the relationship had become strained.

The situation was complex because it had roots that extended way beyond just their relationship. There were the hearts of their respective family members to consider. It affected James's wife and his children.

The trouble was, James felt exploited or taken advantage of by Tom. At first, James was happy to help. But the calls became more frequent. James also started to notice that even though Tom said he was having financial problems, Tom was making new purchases, taking vacations, and didn't seem to be going through a hard time.

James called me because he felt like he needed an outside perspective. This was a case of James starting to reflect on the relationship. The issue wasn't about giving money to a friend; it was whether this was the kind of person he wanted in his life. James didn't want to cast judgment on Tom, but he also couldn't ignore the fact that maybe Tom wasn't someone he wanted to call a friend. I was inclined to agree.

We'll talk more about evaluating a person's "fruit" and interpreting what you see in the next chapter. It's not a perfect science but it is necessary to do as you consider re-aligning someone.

I'm fairly sure that when James called me, he was already aware that the kind of behavior Tom was exhibiting was not something he wanted from someone in his friend category. His questions and concerns were a way to reflect on that. He knew he needed to realign the relationship, but also knew he needed to do it gracefully, in a way that didn't rupture all the other relationships attached to theirs. He would especially need to take some time to think through how to have the conversation he needed while disconnecting from the intimacy he previously had with Tom.

James and I talked about his next steps. He was going to have to set a financial boundary. We came up with some ways to articulate this, using language like, "I'm so grateful I had the opportunity to help you in the past, but because my family is trying to reach some family goals and deal with our own financial issues, I'm unable to assist you financially going forward. I'll be praying for you as you navigate this tough financial season."

Next, James had to decide whether to initiate the communication about that boundary on the front end or have a conversation about that boundary the next time Tom asked him for money. He decided to talk to Tom ahead of time. He didn't want to be emotionally influenced by the nature of the need. If Tom were to call when he was in a real jam, James didn't want that fact to encourage him to violate his boundary.

For James, the way to get some space to reflect, to press pause in the relationship, was to press pause on a specific activity in the relationship. The next challenge was to figure out how to break up the rhythm of the weekly events they were accustomed to attending together. We came up with language to communicate that he had other things he was going to do over the next couple of weeks. And that space gave him the breathing room to make the decision to align Tom differently in his life.

AN ACT OF LOVE

As I mentioned briefly earlier, the idea of aligning people is not a selfish endeavor. I know our culture may suggest it is. Putting people in the right place is not only in your best interest; it's also in their best interest. When God is ordering, guiding, and influencing our relationship decisions, those decisions are always in the best interest of both parties, because God is equally concerned about *both* people in the relationship.

So a decision that I need to make for my best interest will not be to the demise of someone else. Yes, it's entirely possible they may perceive it that way, and it may even feel that way in the short term. But God is a just God. He is not going to create a circumstance that causes me to succeed at someone else's expense.

This doesn't mean that something like that may not occur. It just means that God didn't design it that way. The point to remember, though, is that God is committed to meet our needs, not our preferences. We may have relationships we do or don't prefer, but that is secondary to the relationships we do or don't need. Just as God will send the kind of relationships in my life that I need, God will also send the kind of relationships that I may need to move or remove from my life.

When people are misplaced—put in the wrong categories of our lives—it is not just detrimental for me; it's detrimental for them as well. I'm adversely affected, and they are too. One of the tragic consequences of misplacement that comes from misdiagnosis is this: a relationship that could exist or even thrive on one level becomes so toxic or dysfunctional on another level that it doesn't exist at all. That person who would have been an amazing advisor ends up being a horrible friend, and the relationship dissolves completely. When misplacement happens, some relationships are destroyed that were salvageable. The damage to the relationship becomes so drastic that it is irreparable.

When a person doesn't take the time to reflect, they aren't able to accurately identify the driver of their decisions. Many of us are driven by our feelings, not our faith. Susan David and Christina Congleton talk about "emotional agility" in an article written for the *Harvard Business Review*. According to these leadership experts, "the first step in developing emotional agility is to notice when you've been hooked by your thoughts and feelings . . . Leaders stumble when they are paying too much attention to their internal chatter and allowing it to sap important cognitive resources that could be put to better use."[11]

We also see this all throughout Scripture. Jonah made a decision based on his feelings of not wanting to go to Nineveh. He was angry (see Jonah 1). Naaman didn't want to dip in the river of Jordan because he was filled with pride (see 2 Kings 5).

The point is, when we don't take the time—not just to work *in* the relationship, but to work *on* the relationship, to pause for a moment to reflect and evaluate—we misdiagnose. And misdiagnosis leads to misplacement. Ultimately this means we either move people into different categories, or we end up destroying a relationship that could have been salvaged if we would have placed them properly.

EVALUATION
(FRUIT INSPECTION)

"Every good tree bears good fruit, but a bad tree bears
bad fruit. A good tree cannot bear bad fruit, and a
bad tree cannot bear good fruit. Every tree that does
not bear good fruit is cut down and thrown into the
fire. Thus, by their fruit you will recognize them."

Matthew 7:17–20

Jesus is the ultimate expression of relational intelligence. He
is the most influential figure in human history, and part of
his productivity can be attributed to the way he managed
relationships. He engaged in a practice—one he encouraged
his followers to engage in as well. It's the practice of fruit
inspection. If Jesus says we should recognize people by their
fruit, then he is encouraging us to actually engage in an act of
evaluation.

While *reflection* is an internal exercise, *evaluation* or "fruit"
inspection is an external exercise. It is the act of inspecting the
fruit of the people in one's relational circle and determining

what category the fruit qualifies them for. This exercise should not be confused with making judgments about one's character; rather, it is evaluating your personal experiences with an individual and determining what that means and says to you.

Consider the last conversation you had with, say, your coworker. What did you discuss? Was something said that revealed some aspect of this person's character? How did you feel when you left the conversation? Your evaluation of that person could determine whether that person remains an associate or becomes a friend. Some people aren't bad people; they're just bad *for you*.

ASKING THE RIGHT QUESTIONS

Reflection as it relates to aligning relationships is a thinking exercise. Evaluation, however, is about fruit inspection. In order to evaluate the fruit of someone, we must ask the right questions. Questioning is one of the key ways we get the right clarity to make the right decisions. Right questions give us right clarity. Good questions give us good clarity. When clarity becomes greater, decisions become easier.

One of the first things we must ask actually has nothing to do with another person:

Where am I? Before you can evaluate someone else, it's crucial for us to know what lens we are using. We must ask, In this season of my life, where am I? Where am I emotionally? Where am I spiritually? If we cannot locate ourselves, it will be hard to determine where we want a relationship to go. If we don't know where we are or where we want to go, we won't know who is supposed to go with us.

Based on the answer to this first question, there is a second question to ask:

What do I need? Here's an example that I hope illuminates the importance of this question. I get some of the greatest joy from friends who don't do what I do. They are not in the same line of work. When I engage in conversation with them, I know that the nature of our conversation isn't going to be work-related. So if I'm trying to vacate my mind from thinking about work, they aren't going to inadvertently bring that up because that's not what they do.

There are frequent seasons when I need people in my life who simply are healthy distractions. Of course, that's not *all* the value they add, but these are the kinds of relationships that allow me to disconnect from a world of work that can be all-consuming. So I can answer question one—where am I?—with "I'm in a season where I'm incredibly busy. I have the tendency to be high-strung and overly engaged in work-related activity." I can answer the second question—what do I need?— with, "I need people in my life who add value and who are able to pull me out of the seductive web of work." Then I can make decisions on how to align my relationships.

Relationally, the "what do I need?" question requires some thoughtfulness. We have to ask ourselves what it means to have a certain type of person in our lives. People often speak in generalities. We say, "I need good people in my life. I need good friends." But what does that mean? It's really circumstantial. What is good in one season of our lives may not be good in another. So we need to be specific in identifying our needs.

We should ask ourselves, *What kind of relationships will add the most value to me? What do these people need to be like?*

There's a third critical question to ask in our evaluation process:

What do I have? When I consider those in my relational orbit, in whichever category, it's important to consider what contribution they're currently making to my life. *Currently* is the operative word here. It's easy to think about what someone did twenty years ago and hold on to that. But to address how a relationship has evolved, we must consider what a person is giving us today.

And I know that some people are reading this and thinking, *This sounds so selfish. It sounds so one-sided.* Let me encourage you to see this another way. It's not about being self-centered; it's about stewardship. You must be a good steward of your life and be clear relationally on what you need. We will discuss later what it means to be the kind of friend you want. That is truly another conversation. This is about the kind of value your relationship should add to *your* life.

So once you examine these questions, you will need to draw some conclusions from your answers. If you aren't getting what you need at all, why is that the case? If you're getting a little of what you need, is it possible you have people in the wrong places in your life? This will lead to the final question:

What do I need to do? Does somebody need to be realigned? Does somebody need to be removed? Does someone else need to be pursued?

This is what I've learned. There are some relationships we need to pursue. This is especially true when it comes to the advisor category. If you're in need of an advisor, there are times when that's a relationship you have to pursue. You may even have to initiate that relationship.

THE MYTH IN CHRISTIAN RELATIONSHIPS

Let's be clear, just because two people are Christians doesn't mean they'll have the perfect Christian relationship. That's a myth. That's the inaccurate ideology that many of us operate with. We assume that if both parties love Jesus and love each other, then our relationships will be fruitful. Absolutely not. Just because there are two Christians in a relationship doesn't mean they have a Christian relationship.

The question should never be, "Are we both Christians?" The better question to use in evaluating the relationship is to say, "How are we relating?" It's not that the status of one's salvation isn't important in the dynamics of the relationship. I just mean that relational intelligence goes beyond that.

As Christians, we need to be considerate about the ways we are managing relationships. Can you handle some real talk? There are pastors and first ladies who don't have Christian relationships. There are deacons and deaconesses who don't have Christian relationships. Why? Because relational intelligence is not about the way we worship God, but about the way we *relate* to each other. So in the stage where we're evaluating our relationships and examining fruit, we must especially consider if the "we're both Christians" mantra could be hiding some potential pitfalls: *How does this person relate to me? How do they treat me? How do I treat them?*

AVOIDING JUDGMENT

The dictionary has a number of different definitions for the word *judgment*. Most significantly, it is "the process of forming an opinion or evaluation by discerning and comparing." When we think of judgment in our religious perspectives, it often has negative connotations. But judgment in the way it's actually defined isn't at its core a negative thing.

If we view judgment as the process of forming an opinion or evaluation by discerning and comparing, then, in truth, we're making judgments all the time. I'm forming an opinion about whether I like the food, the clothes, the room, the car.

However, when you talk about judgment in the religious sense of the word, it means something very different. The Scriptures communicate that because only God knows the circumstances and situations people are wrestling with and sorting through, only God is in the position to make the kind of judgments that render a verdict about a person's future or destiny. We are not in a position to do that at all, nor should we ever try.

But we do want to do what the dictionary suggests, which is to go through the process of forming an opinion and then deciding how to proceed based on what we discern. We aren't pronouncing someone good or bad just because they can no longer be our friend. We are simply deciding, based on their actions and character, what's best for our lives. The kind of judgment necessary in this process is about forming an opinion about whether this person is good for you now, not forming an opinion about whether this person is good at all. There is a difference!

It's certainly a fine line, for sure. But if we know we each have the responsibility to determine what would be good for our lives, and we affirm the goodness of any individual, that distinction helps frame the decision. We *all* ultimately have to make our own decisions about the role *all* people will play in our lives.

NEVER DISHONOR THE TREE

Here's the key to all of this: We can inspect someone's fruit without dishonoring the whole tree. In fact, we can inspect someone's fruit without damaging and sabotaging the relationship that's been built so far. Consider the relationship of Jesus and Peter.

It was a Thursday night when Jesus was taken into custody. The Bible says that Peter had been proclaiming and professing his love for and allegiance to Jesus for some time. He felt connected to the Messiah and hadn't hesitated to make it known. Yet Jesus said, "Man, before the rooster crows three times, you will have denied knowing me" (Matthew 26:34, my paraphrase). Sure, Jesus is speaking prophetically here, but he's also communicating something to Peter that he had observed about Peter's character. It's almost as if he's saying, "I've seen a pattern of impulsivity with you, and that's going to play itself out tonight."

I would argue that it is quite possible that Jesus saw this trait in Peter long before he said that to his friend. He likely saw the tendencies of Peter play themselves out along the way. Jesus was able to see something without saying something until it was time to do so, which is a model for how we can approach the period of evaluation. Everything we uncover in our inspection doesn't have to be addressed immediately. Sometimes we see things, and our job is to pray.

Sometimes we say, and sometimes we pray.

It really depends on the level of relationship we have with a person. A person may be an associate, and we may not have the relational equity to say some of the same things to them about what we observe that we would say to a friend. Or a person may be an advisor, and we may not have the emotional equity to say something to an advisor that we would say to an assignment. We should always consider the necessity of our words before moving forward either way.

So inspecting a person's fruit should include honoring them. We should do the best we can in this regard. Because we're imperfect, our inspection will, of course, be imperfect. There may be times when we misinterpret information or when we haven't evaluated something as thoroughly as we should have. If we speak irresponsibly out of an erroneous evaluation, we can cause harm to a person. We can dishonor them and damage the relationship. This is why reflection is the step before evaluation. We have to take the time to process what we've seen or heard. We have to take the time to ask the right questions in order to gain greater clarity and ultimately come to better conclusions.

I remember a time when I was mentoring someone, and the person seemed to be way more interested in being around me than learning from me. While other mentees from time to time would attempt to arrange conference or coaching calls for the purpose of asking specific questions and getting answers, this person was really just highly relational and would constantly ask, "When can we get some time together? Can we hang out?"

I was very close to deciding that this was not going to be a person in my assignment category, because when I looked at some of the criteria I'd mapped out, they weren't being met. This person seemed to desire a kind of relationship I didn't want. But I didn't want to make a knee-jerk decision. I needed to take some time to reflect and pray. I also needed to ask more questions and make sure I was seeing all the information.

One day, for whatever reason, we ended up engaging in conversation, and he began to explain his story. He had a tragic childhood. His parents were on drugs, and he was abandoned as a child. He moved from house to house to house, and the person he thought was his father ended up not being his father after all.

If I had moved on or articulated what I saw in this person without having gained that new information, my words would have been unintentionally but definitely damaging. This young man's backstory gave me a better perspective on what I was seeing. It wasn't about him being relationally needy. His background meant his desire to connect face-to-face was quite normal. This new information meant I could hold my observations and adapt to this person's particular needs as my assignment.

GRACE IN SPITE OF FRUIT

After six days Jesus took with him Peter, James and John the brother of James, and led them up a high mountain by themselves. There he was transfigured before them. His face shone like the sun, and his clothes became as white as the light. Just then there appeared before them Moses and Elijah, talking with Jesus.

Peter said to Jesus, "Lord, it is good for us to be here. If you wish, I will put up three shelters—one for you, one for Moses and one for Elijah."

While he was still speaking, a bright cloud covered them, and a voice from the cloud said, "This is my Son, whom I love; with him I am well pleased. Listen to him!"

When the disciples heard this, they fell facedown to the ground, terrified. But Jesus came and touched them. "Get up," he said. "Don't be afraid." When they looked up, they saw no one except Jesus.

As they were coming down the mountain, Jesus instructed them, "Don't tell anyone what you have seen, until the Son of Man has been raised from the dead."

Matthew 17:1–9

Yes, it is entirely possible to keep a person in certain categories despite their fruit. That's what Jesus did, right? If we were to use the way Jesus arranged his relationships with the disciples, we could say without a doubt that Peter probably shouldn't have been placed in the circle of three on the Mount of Transfiguration. But Jesus *did* draw him in closer. It was an intentional act. The fruit that someone is bearing is not always a reflection of the person they're becoming.

Henry Cloud wrote a book called *Never Go Back* in which he offers wisdom I'll never forget. He writes, "Never go back if the reason that you left in the first place is still there."[12] Cloud is referencing relationships in which we can actively see a person making the attempts to change. This may mean they are gathering the resources and putting forth the effort required to improve themselves or to address and adjust the things they need to.

There are seasons and situations when a person may be exhibiting behavior that is consistent with who they've been, but at the same time, they're putting forth the effort to be a better version of themselves. I don't think we necessarily need to write that person off. Maybe we continue to evaluate them a bit longer. We can ask ourselves, *Is this person putting forth the effort? Are they being resourced properly in a way that demonstrates this is not the kind of fruit they're going to exhibit in the future?*

Even beyond the intellectual exercise of inspecting a person's fruit, I think it's important to listen to your intuition. This is one of the ways God speaks to us. The most intelligent thing a person can do is what God tells them. So while we talk about relational intelligence, we don't want to eliminate the prompting, nudging, and speaking of the Holy Spirit. There are times throughout Scripture when we see God putting people in spaces that are confusing if we were to simply evaluate them with the naked eye.

It's God calling Moses to lead the Hebrews out of enslavement and saying, "I want you to speak to Pharaoh"—and Moses is like, "I'm slow at speech." It's God calling Gideon a mighty warrior when Gideon was threshing wheat in a winepress and there was nothing warrior-like about Gideon's activity. It's Jesus calling Peter a rock when he was flimsy and fragile and impulsive. God sees people with a different set of eyes, and he sees potential where we don't see it. He sees who people are going to become before they become it.

So yes, there are times when we must submit to that other set of eyes. Those divine eyes. There are scenarios where we must give space and grace to people who aren't demonstrating the kind of fruit we need. In these instances, a person who is in the process of becoming who they should become may make us a little uncomfortable. But here's the caveat: their becoming may be frustrating, but it doesn't have to be destructive to us. See, people's growth doesn't have to come at the expense of our well-being. Be sure you are hearing from God when you allow someone to "stick around" who might be demonstrating some rotten fruit behaviors. But also remember that part of being a believer means we sometimes bear people's burdens with them. If their growth simply requires just us being inconvenienced or a little annoyed, I think that's a very reasonable burden to bear.

These kinds of relationships in the meantime must be navigated with grace. Obviously, we need to set boundaries so that nothing dysfunctional, at least that we can control, ends up destroying our lives. We need grace to recognize that our own growth and development has adversely affected other people too. It happens in a marriage, as a parent, with friends, and in many environments. When someone drops the ball, someone has got to pick it up. But wisdom is found in knowing a temporary fumble is not the same as a continuous string of inconsiderate and willfully selfish behavior.

CLARIFICATION

Jesus lived a perfect life. Therefore, he managed relationships perfectly. If there's anyone we're going to learn from in terms of the way to align our relationships, Jesus is an unparalleled and appropriate example. He modeled the management of a relationship circle very clearly with his disciples all throughout the Gospels. His demonstration can offer clarity regarding who goes where in our lives.

As I've noted before, putting people in their place isn't a blessing just to you; it's a blessing to them too. Think about what it will mean to share with a young student—an assignment—the importance of boundaries, of not becoming overly familiar. It's a lesson they will likely carry with them throughout their lives and will be better for it. Designation is not demotion. There is a way to clarify a person's role. In the case of Jesus, he made sure that both "the others" and "the Twelve" always felt like "the Three," even though they weren't.

THE THREE, THE TWELVE, AND THE OTHERS

This concept of the Three, the Twelve, and the others can be implicitly seen in Scripture. In Jesus' relationships, the Three is the category that describes those he was closest to and made the greatest investment in. These were people he had the most intimacy with—he was close to them. In fact, the Three category is what historians called the "inner circle," and these were people who Jesus very clearly managed his relationships with differently than the other disciples (the Twelve).

Then you have the others, which includes the seventy other disciples, as well as other supporters of Jesus' ministry—people who worked and served with Jesus and who were under his influence. Think of Mary, Martha, and Lazarus. Remember in John 11 how Jesus wept when he found out that Lazarus had died? He had great affection for Lazarus. When Mary and Martha sent word to Jesus, he came to intervene. Clearly, Jesus loved these people deeply. Yet he still didn't manage his relationships with them in the same way he managed the inner circle.

The others are people who were in Jesus' relational orbit. Some of these people might have been assignments. Some of them could have been associates. But these were people with whom Jesus had different degrees and different dimensions of relationship. Anyone who doesn't fit into the categories of the Three or the Twelve (which in your life may be the Five and the Fifteen—the number is not set in stone, as it was in the case of Jesus) could be considered the others.

This inner circle of Peter, James, and John was made up of men who, when Jesus went up the Mount of Transfiguration, traveled with him. There he exposed his divinity, the best of who he was, to these three. He did not take the other nine of the twelve disciples. And he did not take people who would fall into "the others" category.

Even when he went to Gethsemane, Jesus took Peter, James, and John. There his humanity was exposed; the worst of his life experience was made plain. He did not take the other nine. Nor did he take the others.

Notice what happened here. He took Peter, James, and John to both the Mount of Transfiguration and the garden of Gethsemane. They experienced his highest point and his lowest point. They apparently were people who could handle that kind of information. These three were safe people. Jesus was showing us how to gain clarity in our relationships here. Whom do we take to our mountains and our gardens? We want relationships with people whose character reveals they are safe enough to handle us when we're at our highest and when we're at our lowest.

Let's say the Mount of Transfiguration represents our high times—moments when we walk fully in our purpose and destiny. Let's also consider the garden of Gethsemane as representing our low times. It represents the exposure of honest emotions. When Jesus was in Gethsemane, he said things like, "Father, if you are willing, take this cup from me; yet not my will, but yours be done" (Luke 22:42). He was in a broken and emotional place—in the kind of agony that only people in the inner circle can handle. People who won't make permanent judgments about who you are based on temporary expressions of your emotions.

The inner circle—in Jesus' case, the Three—are people who don't define your whole book by one chapter. These are people who have enough character to hold you up. They are loyal and trustworthy. They are loving enough to be exposed to you in the garden of Gethsemane and on the Mount of Transfiguration.

No matter whether or not you're religious, we all should have people we judge to be "inner circle" quality. These people are not overly impressed, influenced, or carried away with us at our heights. But they're not overly disappointed with us at our lows. These are people we're safe enough to be vulnerable with. There are some things we only share with certain people because we don't want that information to go certain places.

But here's a point I must make: the inner circle is not perfect.

Peter, James, and John were not perfect. We've already noted how Peter could be impulsive. He could be temperamental. He was arguably loyal. We can write a whole book on Peter's failures—specifically his denial of Christ—and then write a summary of his successes. He had a moment of fear. He acted irrationally. Jesus knew about it, and he predicted it. It didn't stop him from trusting the man. He was clear about Peter's heart.

James and John had their quirks as well. They sat on some serious ambition. They fought about who would get to sit at Jesus' left and right hand. They were not perfect either. Just because we have people in our inner circles doesn't mean these people are absent of imperfections. It just means they meet the character criteria for transparency.

And Jesus' trust was not misplaced. The growth of his ministry and work after his death and resurrection was because of the great intimacy he had with these three. He made a great investment in his friends, Peter, James, and John, who would become influential and consequential leaders in the church.

So what about the rest of the Twelve? They aren't in the inner circle, but they are not exactly in the outer circle either. These were people Jesus did life with. He hung out with them.

They helped him, and he helped them. I would call them "associates," in a sense.

When someone is miscategorized or misaligned, when we haven't put people in their proper place in our lives, we will share "inner circle" information with "outer circle" people—a recipe for disaster, because some "outer circle" people, not necessarily because they're bad people, just are not safe enough to properly manage that information.

We all want to avoid learning on the back end. We don't want to learn the lessons of proper relational placement *after* damage, trauma, and betrayal have occurred.

DISCERNMENT IS THE SECRET

All of these thoughts point back to the need for *discernment* when it comes to gaining clarity about the people we're in relationship with and where they belong in our lives. Discernment is the ability to judge well. It is an essential life skill. The inability to increase our discernment is a key reason we repeat mistakes. We need discernment in all areas of life, especially our relationships. It's a skill that can be improved through experience and experimentation. Our past experiences should be instruments of education that teach us lessons we need to learn in the future.

There will be times when we will see that we've been placing a person in a certain category, and that person never has met or no longer meets the criteria. For example, maybe at one point a person was safe. But they may have recently gone through some experiences that have changed some aspects of their character. Now they're in an unhealthy place and space. As a result, they may not be a safe person with whom to share our highs and lows. This means that a redesignation of their relationship category may be in order.

Please know this isn't a demotion. We aren't passing judgment on the person, nor are we saying, "You are not worthy enough to be in this category." We are saying that at the present time, the person doesn't have the capacity to meet the criteria that the category calls for. And that's okay.

Think of it like this: In the workplace, when a person is a bad fit for a job, no matter how much they want it, it is in their best interest and the company's best interest, that they are reassigned to a place that better suits their gifts. They're going to have less failure in that new place and less of a need for correction. Less failure will likely mean less emotional trauma. The new position will likely cause them less anxiety and will impact their success across the board. When we add up the stress, correction, trauma, and anxiety, along with the lack of productivity, the peace of mind that comes with moving someone to a new position far outweighs all of that.

Now certainly when a person is initially reassigned in the workplace, they're not happy about it. It usually takes some time and requires patience for them to overcome the shock of the transition. Once a person has been operating in the new position for some time, though, they're often able to see the benefits of "being in their lane." That's when they come around. They can now see what they once couldn't and are grateful for the way the move shed light on their gifts. The same goes for people relationally.

However, at times a person doesn't come around to understanding why the relationship has changed. That has to be okay too. Sometimes we not only have to have patience, but we also have to draw boundaries. We have to say to ourselves, *I don't have control over whether or not this person wants a different kind of relationship.* We must be so committed to the best interests of both parties—ourselves and the other person—that if our realignment of the relationship creates a relationship they no longer want, we must respect their choices the same way we want them to respect ours.

ACCEPTANCE

It's one thing to see what we see; it's another to *accept* what we see. The emotional attachment and familiarity one may feel in a relationship is very real, and after reflection, evaluation, and clarification, it can be incredibly difficult to accept what we see. As a spiritual leader, I can say that in my experience this is one of people's greatest challenges. It's difficult for a spouse to accept some things about a partner, a parent to accept some things about a child, a child to accept some things about a parent. Seeing is tough.

But we must.

Maya Angelou once said, "When people show you who they are, believe them."[13] Unfortunately, our emotional attachment to others will sometimes blind us to the reality of where they are in life and whether it's safe for us to be in relationship with them. That college classmate who constantly puts down your dreams of entrepreneurship? That coworker who regularly makes a point to shame you in front of your colleagues? These people are likely not your friends, despite their proximity or the length of time you've known them.

This reality is even more difficult when it comes to families and churches. There are expectations that people have of those who are a part of their natural and spiritual family that don't mirror any other expectations. Spiritually, we expect people's proclaimed values to align with their actual priorities. We expect them to walk what they talk and practice what they preach. We often have higher moral expectations of spiritual family and believe they will be gracious, loving, kind, honest, supportive, affirming, and trustworthy people.

However, there are times when those who claim to know God the best represent him the worst. There are inconsistences and idiosyncrasies that impact us in unpredictable ways. These things can be hard to accept, but we must accept them. Everyone who likes Christ isn't Christlike. This isn't a judgment, nor is it a call to cynicism. It is simply a reality that must be accepted. Just because someone is spiritual doesn't mean they are safe.

This same truth applies to family. We often, rightfully so, have different expectations of our natural family. We expect them to be loving, supportive, and honorable. However, a person's love for us doesn't determine how they treat us. The question isn't whether or not people love us; it's whether or not their love is leading them. There are people who have unaddressed and unmanaged emotional issues that don't allow them to act in loving ways. There are parents who genuinely love their children who also don't act in loving ways, and vice versa.

Just because someone is part of your natural or spiritual family doesn't mean they are safe. What happens when their fruit changes? We are challenged to accept that they may have changed. We struggle with the notion that they may not meet the criteria for elimination, but the relationship certainly is in need of adjustment.

CHOICE MATTERS

Why do we need to spend so much time reflecting, evaluating, and otherwise assessing our relationships? Because who we choose to be in relationship with matters. It's hard to have a good relationship with a bad pick. And sometimes, the first thing we need to accept is that we've made bad choices or have chosen by default. In a Christian context, this must be especially emphasized. It's too easy for church folks to say, "Well, God picks my relationships for me!" This is absolutely not true. Yes, I hear you through the pages. You're pushing back and saying, "No, it's true. God *does* pick. God picked Eve."

No, God didn't pick her. He made her.

God made Eve, yes. He shaped her. He molded and developed her. He fashioned her so that she was right for Adam. So that she was what Adam needed. He developed, and then he presented her. But Adam had a choice whether or not he would choose what was made for him. We can think of it as Adam picked who got picked for him. He picked her over the animals. He picked who God picked for him. But he made the right pick because he was in the right place. He was in Eden, which is a metaphor for unbroken communion and fellowship with God.

We often make bad picks when we're in bad places. This is why asking, "Where am I?" is crucial. That's why being in a bad place in our lives is not the time to establish new relationships.

Because if we're in a bad place, we'll pick somebody that's suitable for that bad place and not for the place we will one day be. But when we grow into a place of health and wholeness, we may look at a person who was good for us back when we were broken but not good for where we are now and say, "I'm supposed to be in relationship with them."

That may not be the case though. That person was supposed to be with us for a season to help us get out of that season, but now that we've gotten some sense, now that we know who we are, now that we're not suffering from rejection, brokenness, low self-esteem, emptiness, and insecurity, our relationships may need to change. This is why we must reject the rebound philosophy, even in friendships and business relationships. "Let me just rebound" means our discernment could be off. Bad picks happen this way, and that's when we may find ourselves saying, "I need God's help."

We often need divine assistance in choosing. Some of us may have a great track record in our choices, but others of us are emotionally healthy enough to honestly assess our past picks and say, "I need God."

Of course, we see the requirement to choose wisely happening all throughout Scripture. God encourages his people to choose what he wants for them, but it is their choice.

If we look at Deuteronomy 30:19, we see this play out. God says, talking to Israel, "This day I call the heavens and the earth as witnesses against you that I have set before you life and death, blessings and curses. Now choose life." In other words, God is saying, "I'm presenting, but you have to choose." And I recognize that today's culture doesn't approach relationships this way. Our culture doesn't always celebrate us being spiritually selective when it comes to whom we engage with. But it is so critical. God would rather that we deal with the pain of loneliness than with the pain of brokenness.

ACCEPTANCE STARTS WITHIN

We all have a few things we need in order to accept what we observe in our relationships. First, we must have a degree of emotional health ourselves in order to define ourselves apart from the relationships we're in. The categories of friend, associate, advisor, and assignment are roles, not identities. I am Dharius Daniels and I am a pastor. I am also a coach, a speaker, a parent, and a husband. These are all roles through which I express different aspects of myself. They are not my identity. I was Dharius before I was all of them, and I don't feel like I can manage any of these roles responsibly if I attach my identity to them. For example, I have to have a sense of worth outside of parenting in order to parent effectively. Otherwise, my sense of self is going to be based on the decisions my child makes.

Relational intelligence is not disconnected from emotional intelligence. Actually, emotional intelligence is a prerequisite for relational intelligence. The whole concept of self-awareness is a key asset when it comes to accepting a new place in a person's life or moving someone into a new place in ours. The degree of emotional health and self-awareness we have is going to determine whether or not a designation feels like a demotion. Whenever there is a breaking of any emotional attachment, it's a loss. With loss, there's going to be grief. All of this is okay. It's essential to be able to grieve the kind of relationship you had, even when that relationship must change. But we have to try to do this from an emotionally stable place.

RESIST RATIONALIZATION

It's easy to rationalize someone's behavior when their fruit changes. We all have done that. We rationalize behavior because we are unable to accept the truth staring us in the face about people we care about. We rationalize behavior because we are aware of our own frailties and want to demonstrate the patience with others that God has given to us. However, we can't allow our rationalizations to get in the way of our realignment.

When we don't see fruit that we should be observing, it can be hard not to rationalize and make up excuses for the person. Sometimes those rationalizations are right. As noted earlier, we may feel compelled to temporarily walk through something with someone. But sometimes—many times—they are wrong. Especially in romantic relationships where there is domestic violence or abuse, or in platonic relationships where there's competitiveness and jealousy, even when we're tempted to come up with reasons why someone is behaving a certain way, it's in our best interest to act on the fruit we see and not the fruit we want to see.

When we allow our rationalizations to become excuses for not making the relational adjustments we should make, it hinders our personal growth because we don't have the right people in the right places in our life. It also hinders that person's growth because it doesn't allow them to come face-to-face with the relational consequences of not dealing with us at the appropriate level.

ALIGNMENT ISN'T A MEASURE OF LOVE

Accepting what we uncover in the reflection, evaluation, and clarification process means we can now begin to align our relationships properly. We must not confuse alignment with love. We don't love people in our group of Three more than we love people in our group of Twelve. We just put people in the Three because at this point in their lives, they're safer than people in the Twelve. However, proper alignment begins with us being clear on some nonnegotiables for our relational categories. For example, in the earlier pages of this book we looked at traits we should look for in friends. In the same sense, we should be clear on traits we cannot accept.

Some traits are so toxic, unhealthy, and dangerous that they shouldn't exist at all in your closest relationships. They include jealousy, competitiveness, abusiveness, and hostility. There is no rationalization for these. Yes, there may be some valid reasons for the presence of this fruit, but as long as these fruits are there, you must adjust the relationship accordingly.

Let's say someone is exhibiting jealousy and competitiveness, and we find out that very real contributing factors came into play in the development of these tendencies. It could be the absence of something, or maybe it's because they didn't get something they should have gotten during their formative years, like affirmation, support, or encouragement. Maybe it's even the result of a traumatic experience where something was taken from them. It could also be insecurity issues, a bad breakup, or emotional abuse.

All of these things are very real contributing factors to why jealousy and competitiveness might show up in a relationship. They are real. And yet no matter what the rationalization, it is not safe to have that person in a position of intimate friendship until they get well. The reason for you to make a decision for adjustment and the way you make this decision may all be influenced by valid reasons but the person cannot be realigned until that fruit has been addressed.

Even when we look in the New Testament, we see the apostle Paul discussing jealousy and competitiveness with the people at Corinth:

> Brothers and sisters, I could not address you as people who live by the Spirit but as people who are still worldly— mere infants in Christ. I gave you milk, not solid food, for you were not yet ready for it. Indeed, you are still not ready. You are still worldly. For since there is jealousy and quarreling among you, are you not worldly? Are you not acting like mere humans? For when one says, "I follow Paul," and another, "I follow Apollos," are you not mere human beings?
>
> What, after all, is Apollos? And what is Paul? Only servants, through whom you came to believe—as the Lord has assigned to each his task. I planted the seed, Apollos watered it, but God has been making it grow. So neither the one who plants nor the one who waters is anything, but only God, who makes things grow. The one who plants and the one who waters have one purpose, and they

will each be rewarded according to their own labor. For we are co-workers in God's service; you are God's field, God's building.

1 Corinthians 3:1–9

Paul is essentially saying, "Man, these issues that you all aren't addressing have relational consequences. They affect people other than you." Sometimes it's only when people feel the reality of those consequences that they are forced to face their issues.

THE SPIRIT OF FRIENDSHIP VERSUS FRIENDS

I'm certainly not saying that just because a person is not in our friend category we aren't friendly with them. The *spirit* of friendship should permeate every relationship—from the associates to the assignments to the advisors. When Jesus talked about his disciples—"I no longer call you servants . . . Instead I have called you friends" (John 15:15)—he is speaking here, in my opinion, about the spirit of friendship.

There is a difference, however, between operating in the spirit of friendship and treating people who are not friends as friends. This can also lead to a kind of unhealthy rationalization. We end up deciding that just because we are friendly with someone that somehow they are our friends.

We also must not confuse alignment with entitlement. There will always be people who feel entitled to certain places and spaces in our life. We may even feel like they are entitled to a particular role because of the nature of the relationship. This could be anything from *we go to church together* to *we are family*. But as I've noted before, just because we are in the same spiritual or natural family does not mean that a person automatically meets the criteria for a particular place or space in our lives. The quicker we can accept this, the better off we can be relationally.

PART 3

Aligning Your Relationships

Relational intelligence not only helps us to accurately define our relationships, but it also helps us align them. Relationship alignment is our responsibility. We are responsible for "putting people in their place." In other words, after we obtain a clear understanding of what category or place the people in our lives are best suited for, we must begin the process of aligning those relationships accordingly.

The hard truth is this: God has called us to certain levels of relationship with certain people. Not with *all* people. He's called us to some of those relationships for certain seasons. Some of those seasons may be longer than others. However, when we recognize that someone has been misplaced or simply needs to be repositioned, we must make the hard decision to adjust the relationship. Honestly, this is where it gets hard for many people. Understanding what needs to be done is one thing; actually doing it is another.

It's not the principles we *learn* that change our lives; it's the principles we *live*. Improving our relational life isn't simply about acquiring information; it's about applying it. In this section of the book, we'll discuss taking the necessary steps to apply what we've learned. We will examine the practices and principles for aligning and realigning our relationships that will take our relationships and lives to another level.

ADVOCATION

My father, Rev. Timothy Daniels, is my hero. I grew up respecting and admiring him. He is undoubtedly the most influential male figure in my life. We had a great relationship as I was growing up, and one of the things I could always do was talk to him about my life—all the things I needed to know and learn. He taught me to play basketball and how to shoot with my left hand. He taught me that the best way to fight was with my brain and not my fists. He also taught me the importance of reading, learning, and studying.

It was my father who taught me how to preach. However, one of the most important and consequential lessons he taught me was to take responsibility for my own life. If I were to borrow the words of Dr. Henry Cloud, I would say that he taught me I am "ridiculously in charge" of my life.[14] He made it clear that I was not to sit around waiting, hoping, and praying that someone else would make decisions that were in my best interest. *I* had to make them. He taught me the importance of advocating for myself.

The word *advocate* is often used to describe the activity of supporting another person or cause. However, relationally intelligent people also advocate for themselves. That's correct! It is important, appropriate, and biblical to advocate for oneself. I would argue that all throughout Scripture, Jesus advocated for himself and encouraged us to do the same. In fact, Jesus was both assertive and proactive when exercising his right to steward his life well. He understood that advocating for his own life was not an infringement on the life or rights of others.

Advocation is not selfishness; it's stewardship. Unfortunately, many people of faith, especially Christians, find this tension difficult to manage. We can often confuse a self-sacrificial life with a self-sabotaging one. In part, this challenge is created by an inaccurate view of Jesus. In my book *Represent Jesus*, I make the argument that there are two Jesuses that exist—the one in our heads and the one in the Bible.[15] The two are not always the same. Until we get Jesus right, we will get *living* like him wrong. Again, Jesus' life teaches us that self-advocacy isn't selfishness; it is stewardship.

REAL STEWARDSHIP

The word *stewardship* is often used in reference to managing financial resources. This isn't necessarily an incorrect understanding of the word, but it is an incomplete one. In truth, stewardship is about properly managing resources, but we must remember that all our resources aren't financial. We have resources related to our energy. We only have so much physical capacity, so we must pay attention to how much we are using. We have resources in terms of our time. Guess what?

Relatively speaking, we don't have much of that either. We also have resources in terms of our skills, competencies, spiritual gifts, and so forth. To some extent, even these have their limitations.

Now consider the human resources you have around you. Think of all the people—individual or collective. It's your human resources that comprise your relationships. And yes, you have to steward those as well.

When it comes to self-stewardship, we must be willing and able to take responsibility for using all of the resources at our disposal in a way that advances God's agenda for our lives. This is essential because others will certainly have an opinion and a preference on how you use all of the resources at your disposal.

For example, a person with some influence will regularly encounter people who have an opinion on how the person should use that influence. However, when a person is really stewarding his or her life, they understand this: "I am responsible for what I'm responsible for and for utilizing the resources at my disposal in a way that advances what I believe to be God's agenda for my life." That's it. This is the only way we're going to see the reality of our desires and God's plan for our lives come to pass. We will be held accountable for how we steward ourselves and the relationships we're in.

Self-stewardship begins with this understanding: *I am responsible for me, and advocating for me is not selfishness; it is stewardship.* You will only see this as selfish if you believe what is in your best interest comes at the expense of what is best for someone else. This is, by far, not true.

Thinking of self-stewardship as selfish also means you believe the only way God can meet the needs of others is through you. It means that in some way you have overestimated your ability and underestimated God's ability to use other people besides you to get other people what they need.

Self-stewardship is especially considered selfish in religious circles. This is because we really try to balance the tension in religious circles between what it means to be a good steward in our own lives and what it means to live sacrificially. Our fate is based on the self-sacrifice of Jesus, and because of that, there is often confusion between selfishness and stewardship when it comes to the Scriptures.

For instance, there is the bedrock command of Jesus: "Love your neighbor as yourself" (Matthew 22:39). He gives the love of self as the frame of reference for how you are to love your neighbor. Essentially, Jesus is telling us that if we get the "self-love" part wrong, we will inevitably get the "love of neighbor" part wrong. In the same way, people reading this text will confuse advocacy with selfishness.

There are certainly times when we must bear one another's burdens, when it is necessary to make a personal sacrifice on behalf of another. But even then, what we sacrifice should not be something that jeopardizes our well-being or our life's purpose. That is not a sacrifice God calls us to make. Too often, people are making these kinds of sacrifices and ending up bitter, frustrated, and confused.

Again, when we believe that what is in our best interest does not have to come at the expense of what someone else needs, we finally understand the difference between advocacy and selfishness. Shifting someone from one category to the next, whether through verbal or action boundaries, may cause discomfort and can certainly come at the expense of what that person may want or prefer, but it will never come at the expense of what either party needs.

This is what is so liberating about self-advocacy. It frees us from the illusion that our welfare and well-being are connected to someone else's behavior. It liberates us from waiting for other people to have epiphanies, lightbulb moments, and revelations about what is in our best interest.

I once coached a client who found implementing some of the strategies in our sessions challenging. She was attempting to take better control of her time and believe that time management is life management. Time is the currency we must be willing to exchange for desired results. Therefore, time management isn't just organizing our time; it is strategically investing it into areas that are going to give us the greatest return. What we do with our time determines whether or not we reach our goals.

This client was an incredibly gifted, goal-oriented, and high-capacity person. However, she could not implement some of the time management strategies she needed to because of the infringement on her time by family members. She was one of the most dependable people in her family, and as a result, her mother and sisters would frequently call on her to help them out in various ways. Many of the issues that allegedly required her assistance were issues that were actually very much avoidable. However, their negligence had become her emergency.

She was speaking with me in our session and venting about how her family was insensitive to all that she had going on. They didn't seem to care about everything she had to go through to manage her life and theirs. I listened to her speak and asked her a question: "Have you ever given your family something you need to go and retrieve?" She paused for a moment, a bit bewildered by the question. She assumed I was speaking of something tangible, like money or possessions. She said, "No." I asked, "Are you sure?" She replied, "I think so."

I asked her permission to give my opinion, and she graciously granted it. I said, "I think you have given your family something God never intended for them to have—control over your life. As your family, they should certainly have influence, but they are not supposed to have control."

It's important to remember the difference between influence and control. The two are not the same, and it's dangerous to confuse them. Whether or not someone has influence or control is not based on what they do; it's based on what we allow. Advocacy keeps us balanced and protected.

INFLUENCE VERSUS CONTROL

Influence is another word that is often abused and misinterpreted. It's entirely possible to have influence with others without controlling them. It's also entirely possible for someone to have influence with you without controlling you. For some people, our words may mean something because maybe we serve on a platform where any number of people choose to listen to what we have to say. There also may be people of influence whom we trust to speak into our lives.

While influence is important, especially when considering how God will utilize it for his glory and our purpose, no one should aspire to use that influence to control and manipulate people. No one should allow themselves to be controlled or manipulated by people who have influence in our lives. The only person we have some degree of control over is ourselves, and if we are going to accomplish a purpose, if we're going to fulfill our life's assignment, if we're going to experience our best life, it can only happen by taking responsibility for ourselves. Responsibility in relationships looks like advocation.

Giving other people control over our lives is like regifting. God has given us the gift of self-control, and we give that gift to someone else. Then we hope the other person manages that gift in a way that is in our best interest. This is not okay. The best thing you can do for the people who are depending on you and the people you want to add value to is to be the best you. My coaching client needed to reclaim the gift of control over her life.

To drive this point home, allow me the opportunity to paint a picture for you. Imagine you're in an advisor-mentee relationship and you begin to feel like your assignment is mismanaging your generosity—whether financially, energetically, or otherwise. We've all been there, right? The assignment has asked for time, coaching sessions, mentoring sessions, lunch, coffee, dinner, or whatever. You've begun to engage with the person, maybe as it relates to professional development and the advancement of their career, and you've shared with them books you think they should read. But over time, you realize that the person isn't reading the suggested books or following up on much of your recommendations. Yet, they're still coming back to you with more requests. How much time and energy will you invest in this person who is clearly not interested in applying any of the guidance that you as their advisor have offered?

Hopefully, not for long!

This is where advocating for yourself is especially necessary. You can certainly wait for that person to stop requesting things from you. But you can also ask that they don't request anything additional until they've actually carried out the previous instructions you've given them. Doing the latter will help you preserve your energy and not waste your time.

Remember that whole thing about managing resources? Time is a precious resource that for so many of us is very limited. Don't find yourself being the person complaining about what someone else is doing in the relationship. Don't be that person who says, "Man, there are so many other things I want to do, but I can't do them because these people are always wasting my time." Don't give away the gift of your time to someone who doesn't know how to properly steward it. One of my mentors often tells me, "Don't complain about what you permit." Step up and advocate for a greater respect for your personal human resources.

CLARITY OF COMMUNICATION

Advocating for yourself does not mean making a demand on what the other person should do. It does mean being very clear about what you are going to do. It means setting boundaries and communicating that, in the case of our previous example, you cannot keep having meetings and investing time with someone if they aren't carrying out some of the instructions you've given.

I've had to recognize the importance of setting boundaries

and embracing advocation in my own life. As a person with his hand in a number of different arenas, I have to be very strategic about the way I utilize my time. I am a pastor of a multisite church with four campuses in three states. I am also an executive coach, an adjunct professor, a speaker, a husband, a dad, and a son.

I believe that God gives us enough time to do all he has *called* us to do, but not necessarily all we want to do. Therefore, if we properly steward and manage our time, we will be able to faithfully steward the responsibilities God has given us. In light of that, I have to be very selective with how and where I invest time. I only take meetings I believe are necessary, and those meetings have to start and end on time. I limit the number of coaching clients I take on and will only maintain the coaching agreement with those who actually demonstrate a desire to do what it takes to get better.

I've learned that if I waited for everyone else to discern what was in the best interest of my time, I would mismanage all the things God has given me stewardship over. My family would suffer; my health would suffer; my clients would suffer; my students would suffer; and my church would suffer. I have to set boundaries in order to be and experience God's best. I have to advocate for me.

Another place where these kinds of advocacy decisions have to be made and communicated is on the job. Many of us have found ourselves having to make clear to a coworker that there isn't a friendship between us and them. This is one of those circumstances where verbal communication of this fact may or may not be necessary. Some situations will require clear verbal boundaries ("I'm not comfortable with us going there yet, so I'd rather not discuss that"), and other scenarios will require boundaries that are nonverbal (stopping the person from sharing a personal story, not hanging out at the coffee shop after work).

This is something you'll need to discern on a case-by-case basis. The categories of friend, associate, assignment, or advisor are for *you*—a way for you to organize how you will engage with the person—not necessarily for the other person. We talked about discernment in previous chapters, but it's especially important as you think through whether a coworker is an associate relationship, where merely the spirit of friendship is appropriate, or whether the associate is becoming a true friend.

TYPES OF COMMUNICATION

Jesus said to his disciples, "You're no longer my servants; you're my friends" (John 15:15, my paraphrase) but they were still his apprentices, his mentees. He is demonstrating that there should absolutely be a spirit of friendship that permeates every relationship. This will show up as being considerate of a person's time, being cordial, showing empathy, and having an overall sense of camaraderie. But as I've noted, this is different from the friendship category. And while the spirit of friendship will show in associate, assignment, and advising categories, the dynamics of these categories are very specific.

But here's the thing: in most cases, the presence of a spirit of friendship does not necessarily mean we have to announce to a person the category they're in. In fact, the categories don't come first at all. We should not categorize a relationship and then try to make it that. We should be discerning and assess the relationship as it currently is, and then call it what it is.

Communication is important, but the type of communication will vary, depending on the category and circumstance. There may be a reason it wouldn't be necessary to verbalize to a person, "This isn't what you think it is." What is necessary is simply advocating for the kind of relationship you want by setting boundaries when you feel like that person is pushing the relationship in a direction you don't want it to go.

VERBAL BOUNDARIES

We'll dive more into this in a later chapter, but boundaries don't always have to be verbalized, but they do have to be implemented. There are occasions when we might see a person is dealing with an offense or isn't reading our queues and is consistently and assertively attempting to push the relationship further, and we need to have a conversation.

To handle this, we need to do something that some will find controversial. See, I always believe in telling the truth. We should speak the truth in love to that person. But—and this is the controversial part—we must discern *what* truth to tell.

Let's say there's someone in your life who's an associate. They'd like to be your friend, but for whatever reason you don't consider them safe. There's a way to communicate to that person that this is not the kind of relationship you're looking for without actually saying, "Well, you know, you don't seem to be trustworthy. You talk to me about other employees. I don't feel comfortable having a relationship with you in that regard."

It's not that this isn't true, but we really should consider whether sharing those observations is necessary for someone we aren't close to. The level of relationship we have determines the kind of permission we're given to be transparent with that person.

So no, we should never be deceptive. It is important, however, when verbalizing a boundary, to know what part of the truth to tell a person. I've had some of my best and most enlightening experiences with this while working with sports coaches. In another life, I was an NBA basketball player who was the starting point guard for the Philadelphia 76ers (the best fans in the world). In real life, I was an average point guard who played *a little bit* at a Division III college in Mississippi.

However, during my time playing ball, coaches always had to have hard conversations with players. In order for a player to improve, the team to win, and the coach to succeed, they had to tell the truth. My coaches were always strategic about what part of the truth to tell. For example, during my first two years, I was very athletic but not a great shooter. My coach, John Stroud, knew that if I improved my shooting, it would not only greatly increase my effectiveness as a player but would also help us out as a team.

I will always remember how he framed his critique. He didn't bring me into the office and say, "Dharius, your shooting sucks. You can't shoot a rock into an ocean. Teams know you can't shoot, and that's why they don't guard you close." Those words would have been true, but his goal wasn't to have a venting session. He was seeking to help me improve, not dump on me.

People aren't trash cans and they shouldn't be subject to us dumping our emotional garbage on them. Unfortunately, this isn't necessarily reflective of the way many business leaders, spiritual leaders, coaches, and parents attempt to motivate people. They erroneously assume that just because people *accepted* the way something was said, they *embraced* what was said. There is a difference. The dumping approach often demotivates the person and destroys morale.

My coach's goal was to improve me as a player without doing unnecessary damage to me or to our relationship. Therefore, our conversation was something more like this: "Dharius, you are an important part of our team. You are the quickest guard we have, and we need you to get better. If you improve your shooting, you'll be very difficult to guard and it will free up our other players to thrive in their positions too. So this off-season, I want you to really work on your shooting." That's exactly what I did, and I came back a much more balanced and well-rounded player.

Coach Stroud told me the truth, but he knew what part of the truth to tell me. As a coach, he had a responsibility to do his job. That job was to get the best out of his players and put the best players on the court. However, he was able to advocate for his calling without destroying me and our relationship because he knew how to tell the truth and what part of the truth to tell. So remember, it's not that we should avoid telling "hard truths." I'm saying that all truth doesn't have to be hard.

CONVERSATION

Once a person has embraced the fact that it's okay to engage in advocation, they are ready for the next step, which is conversation. More often than not, whenever there is a discovery, an epiphany, or a revelation, the next step is to have a conversation with the person or persons involved. When a parent discovers something about their child, the next step is a conversation. When a coach discovers something about a player, the next step is a conversation. When we discover something about a relationship, the next step oftentimes will be a conversation.

As introduced in the previous chapter, it is not necessary to announce every relational adjustment one makes. There are some changes we will make that won't require "breaking news" announcements. There are times when we can make adjustments without communicating it. This is usually because the adjustments are small, subtle shifts that will likely result in people not necessarily knowing the difference. If there is a situation where there is limited engagement with a person and we decide we need to make a shift in the nature of that relationship, that shift may not warrant a conversation. However, there are other scenarios where we must engage in some kind of conversation.

These types of conversations are often expressions of the Golden Rule. They are an opportunity to "do to others as you would have them do to you" (Luke 6:31). In the case of a friend who no longer meets your personal criteria for friendship, it's highly likely that they will be owed some kind of conversation. When it is time to have a conversation with those in our lives who may be moving from one category to another, we should start with preparation. We must prepare ourselves for the conversation, as well as prepare ourselves for the reactions. It's critical to know when to speak and what to say when we do.

SOME MOVES MATTER MORE

The conversations in which we shift people in one direction may absolutely be easier than a conversation shifting people in another direction. If a person is going from an associate to a friend, that conversation is easier to initiate and easier for other people to hear. However, moving someone from assignment to associate or from friend to associate may be much more challenging. This is why we must be emotionally prepared when initiating a category-shifting conversation. We must be prepared for any emotional blowback we may receive and any guilt that may arise. In fact, we are likely to feel a variety of emotions.

Our degree of emotional intelligence will really be a driver in how well we handle the conversations we need to have. When Peter Salovey and Jack Mayer developed the theory of emotional intelligence in 1990, they essentially posited that "emotions had a marked impact on an individual's thinking and behavior."[16] Robin Stern, associate director for the Yale Center for Emotional Intelligence, continues the work of refining what emotional intelligence is.

In an article published on CNN.com, Stern is quoted as saying, "Emotional intelligence is being smart about your feelings. It's how to use your emotions to inform your thinking and use your thinking to inform your emotions." She continues by saying that "some people think of emotional intelligence as a soft skill or the ability or the tendency to be nice. It's really about understanding what is going on for you in the moment so that you can make conscious choices about how you want to use your emotions and how you want to manage yourself and how you want to be seen in the world."[17]

When having a conversation where it feels like a person needs to move from being a friend to an associate, it's incredibly important to always remember that we are having these conversations because of what's going on with *us*, not necessarily what's going on with *them*. There certainly may be things you see in them that may have precipitated a move, but when we're having the conversation, our position must come from the perspective of what we need and not necessarily who they are not.

One way to frame this is to say, "I greatly value our relationship and the contributions you've made to my life. You're one of the most significant and important people in my life. You've probably noticed over the past couple of months or so that things have been different with me. There are some things I've just been thinking through and reassessing in my own life.

I am recalibrating and refocusing for the future. As a result, I feel like I must make some adjustments in my relationships right now."

Remember, it's important to not make accusations. There are no "you didn't do this and that's why I can't be friends with you" statements. The focus is on the needs of the person initiating the conversation and the move that needs to be made. The reason this approach is important is it reduces the likelihood of us making a judgment about the life of the person we are reassigning. That person may have evolved in ways that are unhealthy for us, but it doesn't always mean it's wrong for them. When we position the shift as more about where *we* are and not where *they* are, it keeps the conversation about us simply stewarding our own lives and not necessarily judging theirs.

Another way to position this could be, "I've been throwing myself so much into my career [or family]. I've been trying to spend some time developing myself, doing some self-improvement. Because of that work, I've had to shift the way I relate to you and the nature of our relationship. I just want you to be aware of that. I want you to know that as I sort through this, my time is going to be limited. I won't be able to spend as much time doing some of the things we used to do. I'd really appreciate and value you being a part of my life. I hope I have your support as I sort through what life looks like for me in this next season."

The focus of these category-shifting conversations should be on communicating how some of the interactions will change and not necessarily on assigning a new identity to the person. Language is incredibly important, so communicating how we are going to relate to a person differently as opposed to requesting them to relate to us differently is paramount. Remember, we are advocating for *ourselves* only. There are times when we may feel like people have changed when they haven't; we are the ones who have changed. That's why it's critical when we're having these conversations to communicate what's going on with us. Sometimes we don't realize that the person we need to converse with is being who they've always been, and it's only we who see things differently.

The conversation that occurs when a person is moving from associate to friend is very different because of the relational proximity that changes. The tone will likely be different, as well as the emphasis. We are asking someone to come closer. As a result, we are placing high value on *who* they are more than what we need. When we are moving someone away from us relationally, we make the conversation about us. But when we are pulling them close, the conversation is about them. This requires some vulnerability on our part. Pulling close means we are acknowledging our need for someone else and exposing ourselves to the possibility of being rejected. However, the payoff of the right person being in the right place in our lives far exceeds the risk of rejection.

We should not allow fear to become a fetter that imprisons and ensnares us, keeping us from making the kind of requests that can bless our lives and accelerate our advancements. We must be courageous enough to make the ask! When I reflect on the most significant relationships in my life, they have been relationships I've had to pursue. We would be surprised at who may mentor us if we would just ask. We would be surprised to see who may help us if we would just ask. We would be surprised to see who may offer us opportunities if we would just ask. That's why we must have the courage to have these kinds of conversations.

Here's an example of how that conversation could go: "We've been working together for ten years. I've had the opportunity to get to know you, and you're an incredible person. You're trustworthy, you're kind, etc. I'm in a season when I've been seeking friendships. I don't want to make any assumptions about the way you view our relationship, but I do want you to know that I see you that way, and I would love to develop a friendship with someone like you."

Another way to approach moving someone closer, say, from assignment to friend, is this: "I think we've moved past the point of me just pouring out my expertise for your own personal development. You've shown yourself to be a person who is trustworthy and genuine, and I feel like it would bring me great joy to have you in my life as a friend. I don't know where you are in life, what all you have going on. But I did want to communicate what I felt, just in case you felt the same thing and would be open to that. I would love to continue pursuing a friendship with you."

So in sum, when we are drawing people closer to us, shifting them into the more intimate category of friendship, the emphasis in our conversation should be on honoring them and illuminating the characteristics in them we most admire. We should also share how we'd like someone with those values and traits to be a part of our life. Some people may argue that these types of conversations are unnecessary. I strongly disagree. Conversations like these help clarify expectations. A large amount of frustration in many relationships boils down to misplaced expectations. When conversations are had, expectations are clarified.

ACQUIRING AN ADVISOR

One of the most difficult conversations to have is when we are attempting to bring an advisor into our lives. At some point, we will all need advisors or mentors of some sort. Inviting a mentor into our space is very similar to inviting a person into the friendship space. What needs to be clearly communicated to them are the traits we find admirable, where we are in our lives, and how that person can add value in significant ways.

Here's a potential way to broach that conversation: "I've watched you from afar. I've learned so much from watching you. I know someone like you is incredibly busy and has great demands on you. But I would be honored and fortunate if, in some way, you could serve as an advisor or mentor in my life. We can discuss what that looks like for you. I'm open to different forms."

Being open to the various ways in which a person is willing to serve in this role is important. Approaching situations with an "all or nothing" mentality is dangerous because it can suggest that we have an attitude of entitlement. When we're requesting someone to invest their time, energy, and knowledge into us, we must be open to them doing it in ways that work best for them.

Forbes provided some helpful insight on the various ways to secure a mentor or advisor. One point that stood out in the article, "4 Tips for Finding Great Career Mentors," was the idea that we need to clarify what we want upfront:

Clarify what you want. Before seeking out mentors, write down your specific expectations and the role you want mentors to play in your career. Do you want someone who can help your stalled networking attempts, assist you in learning more about a certain industry or provide guidance on how to be a successful entrepreneur? Clarifying your expectations, goals and objectives will ensure you find the right mentors and that the relationships benefit your professional goals.[18]

This applies in the professional realm of our lives, but it's just as applicable when seeking personal development and spiritual mentors.

Another approach is this: "If I'm honest, what I've seen in you—your example, competence, exposure, and capabilities—is something that could probably save me years. It could help me tremendously. I would truly be honored if you'd consider exploring the possibility of developing a mentoring relationship with me. I'm flexible enough to be open to the different ways that something like this has to flesh itself out. But I would really love to have you in that space in my life."

WHAT'S NEEDED MOST:
COURAGE AND LOVE

At the root of all these conversations is *courage*. For every level and every variation in these conversations, there is a degree of courage needed. It takes courage to push someone further away. It takes courage to invite someone in. It's one of the reasons emotional intelligence truly is the foundation for relational intelligence. It's our emotional intelligence that will allow us to overcome all of the competing emotions that we feel when it comes time to sort through these things.

In addition to courage, *love* must drive these conversations. We must hold love in our hearts, whether we are pushing away or inviting in. In the case of the former, speaking the truth in love is not just about not hurting someone's feelings; it's about being a decent human being who lives life with some level of empathy. We all need someone who can tell us about ourselves. Someone we trust who ultimately has our best interests at heart. Someone to whom we can say, "I know you're saying this to me because you love me, not because you're trying to control me." When compassion shows up in the conversation, compassion drives the conversation, even when it's incredibly hard.

It's so important to empathize with the person who is sitting in the other seat. It doesn't even matter if the reason we are, say, putting distance between us and the other person is that some issues are going on with them, that there are some imperfections they're attempting to address, we must still place ourselves in their shoes and consider how the conversation will impact them—even as we proceed with it.

Scripture teaches that when we are engaging in relationships, even if we are making a correction, we should absolutely sit in the seat called empathy. In his letter to the Galatians, Paul writes that when we're restoring someone, we should be doing so in the spirit of meekness (see Galatians 6:1). We should always ask, *How would I want this conversation to be had if I were sitting where that person is sitting?*

So right or wrong, up or down, love is always the best

delivery system for truth. It's truth's transportation system. And here's the thing—not telling someone the truth in love will likely cause more damage to people emotionally than a moment or two of hurt feelings. Even if the response to the conversation is deeply emotionally reactive, we cannot be imprisoned by a person's feelings.

Yet we do need to be considerate of those hurt feelings. In many cases, hurt feelings can reveal so much more. Hurt feelings can reveal wounded souls. Too often, rejection is tattooed on people's hearts already, and this conversation may be a trigger for that. Sometimes a negative response reflects an increase in insecurity or a diminished self-esteem as a result of the perceived rejection. People are affected in many ways that go beyond feelings.

PREPARING FOR THE AFTERMATH

When we receive a negative response to our conversations, it can be easy to want to back down. We may even be inclined to change our minds. It's tough to stay the course in the face of disruption in a relationship. But part of how we deal with the aftermath of a tough realignment conversation has to do with what we do before we even have the talk. We must prepare. We must ask, *How can I ready myself for the emotions I could potentially feel when this conversation is had?* We must allow ourselves to consider how to brace ourselves for the reactions from the other person that could make us feel worse about something we already feel bad about.

When it comes to emotional preparation, it's not about

predicting how you're going to feel. That's not something we can anticipate in many cases. However, we can prepare ourselves for how we are going to react.

For me, preparation involves jotting down some notes. This allows me to think through the potential reactions I could get. It looks a little like this:

This person could be upset.
They may cry.
They may be offended.
They may leave.
They may talk behind my back later on.

Now, as I said, there's often no way to determine how I will *feel* if any of these should happen. But I can think through how I will react. Practically, I can consider how I'm going to respond to each potential reaction. I will also need to think through whether there may be any situation in which I could change my mind. That is particularly true in a business relationship. We may be getting ready to let someone go, and it is crucial to know ahead of time if there is any scenario in which when we walk into that room, we could see ourselves changing our minds.

Examining those scenarios ahead of time gives us time to work out the best approach and to even circumvent any backtracking we may be inclined to do. It allows us to focus on moving forward with a decision that is in our best interest. It helps us stay the course. If simply writing down the various outcomes is wrecking us emotionally now, it could be an indication of something else that needs our attention. Oftentimes, we want to avoid having these conversations out of fear of causing or feeling pain. However, waiting often exacerbates the pain both parties experience in the future and could rupture the relationship in a way that's beyond repair. It may be an indication we need to engage in some inner healing and may be suffering from what I call "rejection infection."

THE REALITY OF REJECTION

Rejection can come to us for many reasons, including when someone has "read" us inaccurately or misinterpreted our actions and relational posture. Everyone has experienced it personally and professionally. However, when rejection is not properly dealt with, it can produce a wound to our soul that affects our sense of self. A soul wound is dangerous because the bleeding is internal and invisible. These kinds of wounds are often underestimated and overlooked. They are treated in a way that is consistent with what the Old Testament prophet Jeremiah describes:

> "They dress the wound of my people
> as though it were not serious.
> 'Peace, peace,' they say,
> when there is no peace."
>
> *Jeremiah 6:14*

When we don't take soul wounds seriously, we end up putting Band-Aids in places that actually need stitches. You may be aware of what happens to unaddressed wounds. The wounds become open to infection. Infections from rejection don't always show up in the form of pain. They often show up in the form of personality traits that we incorrectly associate with our identity. We say things like, "This is just the way I am." In truth, just because we are a certain way doesn't mean we are supposed to be that way. Just because this is the way we have been doesn't mean this is the way we have to be. Apathy, timidity, and the inability to have hard conversations can be an indication that we have some rejection infection. Therefore, these aligning conversations are not only good for the relationship; they are also good for us. They expose areas of our own lives where we may need to grow. In fact, these conversations facilitate our growth.

Do not delay the inevitable. Reframe the pain, not as a deterrent, but as a motivator. We can say, "Because this sucks, because this is going to hurt, because this is uncomfortable, let me go ahead and get this done and get it out of the way." Use the pain to continue the course as opposed to an excuse for not doing what needs to be done. Putting off the realignment conversations we need to have with the people in our lives only hurts more in the long run.

LIMITATIONS

I have some news you may or may not find surprising.

Everyone doesn't listen.

We shouldn't make the assumption that once someone has heard our aligning conversation, they will act accordingly. We may at times find ourselves in situations where people simply don't understand what we are saying or where they don't agree and refuse to give us the space we have requested. Therefore, this next step is extremely important.

After we've had conversations, we must set some *limitations*. We must establish boundaries. Jesus, who is the greatest expression of relational intelligence, models this masterfully: "Immediately Jesus made the disciples get into the boat and go on ahead of him to the other side, while he dismissed the crowd. After he had dismissed them, he went up on a mountainside by himself to pray. Later that night, he was there alone" (Matthew 14:22–23).

Jesus certainly had a unique bond with his disciples, but at the same time he knew when to establish boundaries with them. He sent them away so he could go to the mountainside to pray. He knew he needed to create some space to replenish himself spiritually, physically, and emotionally, and he couldn't do that with the disciples around. In order to help them, he needed to set boundaries with them.

There are other examples where Jesus got away from crowds, instructed people to keep some miracles private, or went to solitary places for times of replenishment. He set limits. He didn't wait for his followers to have an epiphany about what he needed. He practiced the art of setting boundaries.

To be clear, boundaries aren't about what others will and won't do; boundaries are about what *you* should and shouldn't do.

DEFINING AND MODELING BOUNDARIES

Let's revisit Henry Cloud and John Townsend's work for a moment as we dig deeper into boundaries. In their book *Boundaries*, they help us understand their importance:

> Boundaries define us. They define *what is me* and *what is not me*. A boundary shows me where I end and someone else begins, leading me to a sense of ownership.
>
> Knowing what I am to own and take responsibility for gives me freedom . . . Taking responsibility for my life opens up many different options . . .
>
> Boundaries help us distinguish our property so that we can take care of it. They help us to "guard our heart with all diligence." We need to keep things that will nurture us inside our fences and keep things that will harm us outside. In short, *boundaries help us keep the good in and the bad out . . .*

Setting boundaries inevitably involves taking responsibility for your choices. You are the one who makes them. You are the one who must live with their consequences. And you are the one who may be keeping yourself from making the choices you could be happy with . . .

Our minds and thoughts are important reflections of the image of God . . . *We must own our own thoughts . . . We must clarify distorted thinking.*[19]

Boundaries are guidelines. They come in the form of rules and barriers. They are the limitations we set regarding what we will permit or allow in the context of a relationship. The purpose of boundaries is not necessarily to control what someone else does, but it is to limit and protect us from the impact their activity has on us. Boundaries are our way of determining what we will tolerate, what we will permit.

Establishing boundaries begins with accurately understanding what boundaries are, understanding that we cannot use our boundaries to control or manipulate another person. One of the greatest mistakes people make in attempting to adjust a relationship is communicating to other people what *they* need to do in order for a boundary to be lifted. Again, that is manipulation.

For instance, maybe you're relating to a person who has shown they're not trustworthy because they've exposed aspects of your life without consent. Maybe it's a work environment where the culture and ethics of the office require confidentiality and this person has broken that trust by communicating what should be confidential. Boundaries won't stop that person. Boundaries don't make others trustworthy or honest. They don't make a person who is compulsive more disciplined.

I know. That sucks, right?

What boundaries will do, though, is protect you from the impact of that person's dishonesty, compulsiveness, and so forth. So you set a boundary to ensure you will never tell them anything personal or intimate. The nature of that boundary doesn't change how they act, but it does reveal to you the nature of the relationship. This person is an associate. They should only be engaged in the context of work and only when absolutely necessary. This isn't a friendship, and setting the boundary helps reveal that fact. This distinction is critical for your own emotional safety and peace of mind.

In relationships where the access one has to someone and the time one spends with a person are already limited, boundaries become a bit easier to set. If we don't work together, if we don't worship together, if we don't live together, then it's easier for me to remove myself completely from your space. But this changes with proximity and engagement. If we work together, worship together, etc., setting boundaries can be much more challenging. Nevertheless, it must be done. If a coworker proves to be untrustworthy, the way we set a boundary is really simple—refuse to give them access to information we don't want exposed. This will ultimately limit the conversation we *do* have with the person.

Now let's say you make this shift. You've started setting boundaries but have chosen to not have a conversation about it. You simply stop engaging with the person on topics related to your personal life. This person may notice the shift and ask about it. Be ready for that, and then revisit chapter 10. This has now become an incredible opportunity to speak the truth in love to that person—from the perspective of what *you* need and not necessarily any of their imperfections. We can hope that this may have been simply a blind spot for them, a flaw that needs to be addressed so it won't keep costing them relationships the way it cost them in your relationship.

Here's a way to frame setting a boundary or limitation with a person: "You know, sometimes I like to share certain personal aspects of my life. But those things need to be kept secret so I can feel safe. I need to be comfortable knowing this is taking place. For whatever reason, I haven't felt the kind of confidence I need to. So because of that, I'm thinking through how best to respond and whether I have to make some adjustments in our relationship for my own peace of mind." Notice that the framing of this is still focused on *your* needs in setting the boundary. It isn't condescending or accusatory, but it still addresses the issues and sets the limits.

Sometimes setting a boundary is a proactive or preemptive move. It could be about refusing to expose information about ourselves to a person in the first place. Let's say there's a person who is insulting, belittling, and condescending toward you. Remember, there is no boundary you can set that will change that person. You can't make a condescending person more empathetic. But what you can do is set a boundary in terms of how much of yourself you are willing to expose to that person. You can limit how much access you are going to give them on the front end.

A way to frame this could be, "For my own emotional health, I'm trying to focus more on my relationships. I want to have a positive perspective on life because it's way too easy to beat myself and my family up. I want you to know, though, that it's really hard to do these things if I feel like I'm being talked down to and insulted. There have been times I've felt this way with you, and I want you to know how it makes me feel. I know I have to make adjustments to our relationship so it stops happening."

Importantly, if this person is abusive or combative in a way that makes you uncomfortable, you're going to have to remove yourself from the room. Doing that is not disrespectful; it is what's necessary to preserve your mental, emotional, and physical health. Remember, self-care isn't selfishness; it's stewardship.

MANAGING THE RESISTANCE

We are often resistant to the idea of setting boundaries mostly because of our need for validation. Setting boundaries means we won't always be liked by our friends, especially those we connect with primarily via clicks culture, and this can be problematic for many of us.

For people of faith, the resistance comes from a misunderstanding of what God has called our relationships to be and do. We too often have this flowery perspective on what it means to live in a way that is self-sacrificing, based on false teachings and misinterpretations of Scripture.

In both cases, the resistance boils down to many of us struggling with our pleasing tendencies. Our need to please people, to be liked, is very often a symptom of someone who has been dealt rejection or lived with an absence of affirmation. And one of the things that ends up happening is we don't set boundaries and end up with many misaligned relationships.

There are times when people would rather deal with the pain of no boundaries than the emotional reaction from people when they set them. And yes, some of that is fear. We are afraid of how people are going to react and respond. Putting people in their proper place reminds us that there are people in our lives who probably shouldn't be there. And the idea of that is scary.

We have to work through the fear of losing relationships in our own minds so that fear isn't what drives our decisions to resist realigning folks. Instead of being afraid of what will happen if we realign a relationship, we should probably take an approach that says, "I'm going to shift my thinking to being afraid of what will happen if I *don't* realign this relationship."

THE ROLE OF DIGITAL ACCESS

In the age of social media, it's seemingly more difficult to set boundaries than in the past. Part of this is because social media gives us increased access to people that we wouldn't normally have access to. Becky Sweat, a writer for *Discern* magazine, wrote about the impact of our digitally driven world on building relationships:

> In many ways, our modern lifestyles actually work against friendship. Just about everyone is overbusy, overstretched and overscheduled. Between work, classes, household chores and family commitments, there isn't a lot of time left to develop or nurture friendships. Small talk with coworkers or text messages to say "hi" may be all we manage to fit in.

To be sure, even brief interactions can brighten our day. Yet God created us to need more than just superficial social ties. We need true, biblical friendships.[20]

That said, social media also makes it difficult to set the kinds of boundaries necessary to sustain those friendships.

With email, I can choose who I give my email address to. With my phone, I can choose who I give my phone number to. With my home, I can choose who I give my address to. None of this is true on social media. Even with the most stringent security settings, if someone wants to find us, they generally can. That access may present a false sense of community that can have people sitting in categories of our lives unjustifiably.

Social media does offer another layer for someone to reach you, but that layer is thin because of the amount of information we provide to our social media accounts. All that being said, social media isn't the problem. It's us. We can get in our own way. Our inability to handle the emotional consequences that can come from shifting our relationship is the driving factor as to why we don't set the boundaries we may desperately need.

ELIMINATION

Repositioning is not always possible when aligning your relationships. There are some cases where a relationship is so unproductive or unhealthy that the person needs to be eliminated from your relational orbit. In other words, there are times when people can be repositioned and there are times when people have to be removed.

If we assume that the people in our lives are always supposed to be a part of our lives, it is likely we have an unrealistic and romanticized view of relationships. This view can be dangerous for our lives and business. There are times when a relationship has to end. Unfortunately, some dating relationships have to end. Some business partnerships have to end. Some friendships must end. When we come to that fork in the road, we must have the intelligence to make the hard call.

I want to begin by saying you cannot do this step right if you view it wrong. Handling and executing this step will require viewing it through the proper lens. Elimination is probably the most difficult consideration for most of us. Most of the reasons it's hard to practice elimination have to do with the way we perceive eliminating someone from our lives. It's often seen as unloving, rash, or even cruel. Depending on the kind of relationship we may have had with the person we need to eliminate, we may feel we are abandoning an individual by failing to invest in them. The knowledge of having to eliminate someone from our lives can evoke feelings of guilt, shame, and obligation.

Also, there are times when we don't want to eliminate someone who needs to be eliminated because we recognize that the person doesn't *only* bring negative things into our life. Maybe there's some value this person adds that we don't want to lose. The dissolution of the relationship between Saul and David post-Goliath helps with this:

> The king [Saul] said, "Find out whose son this young man is."
>
> As soon as David returned from killing the Philistine, Abner took him and brought him before Saul, with David still holding the Philistine's head.
>
> "Whose son are you, young man?" Saul asked him.
>
> David said, "I am the son of your servant Jesse of Bethlehem . . ."
>
> From that day Saul kept David with him and did not let him return home to his family . . .
>
> Whatever mission Saul sent him on, David was so successful that Saul gave him a high rank in the army. This pleased all the troops, and Saul's officers as well.
>
> When the men were returning home after David had killed the Philistine, the women came out from all the towns of Israel to meet King Saul with singing and dancing, with joyful songs and with timbrels and lyres. As they danced, they sang:

"Saul has slain his thousands,
and David his tens of thousands."

Saul was very angry; this refrain displeased him greatly.
"They have credited David with tens of thousands," he
thought, "but me with only thousands. What more can he
get but the kingdom?" And from that time on Saul kept a
close eye on David . . .

When Saul realized that the LORD was with David and that
his daughter Michal loved David, Saul became still more afraid
of him, and he remained his enemy the rest of his days . . .

Saul told his son Jonathan and all the attendants to
kill David.

1 Samuel 17:56–58; 18:2, 5–9, 28–29; 19:1

As this story demonstrates, Saul was very fond and complimentary of David initially. However, Saul's fondness eventually
turned into jealousy when David defeated Goliath. As we read
on, we notice that Saul becomes competitive and even physically violent with David. This was certainly a relationship
that David needed to eliminate. However, there were aspects
of the relationship that made it difficult for David to do so.
Saul was a fatherlike figure to David, and in that way, David
was benefiting relationally from his relationship with Saul. In
addition, David was very blessed by the "employment opportunity" Saul had provided. It blessed him financially and put him
in a position to bless his family. Eliminating this relationship
meant he would also eliminate some things that were positive.
I'm almost certain he had some reservations and hesitation.

We all do this. When we find ourselves in situations like

David's, where a relational break could cause complications, it's easy to resist doing what needs to be done. People in toxic relationships will frequently say things like, "It's not all bad." People in business environments may make justifications like, "Maybe I haven't trained them enough" or "I don't want to just abandon them." All of these are valid feelings. However, we should make sure these feelings flow from empathy and introspection and not from a faulty view of elimination.

This is something I struggled with for a vast part of my life. It hurt me and our organization in a number of ways for years. For years, I struggled with the idea of eliminating people, believing it was being unchristian to do so. I felt like God and many others had been so incredibly patient with me that I wanted to demonstrate the same kind of patience to others. I felt like it was what the Scriptures required of me. Therefore, when it came to my leadership of our organization, I allowed people to stay in roles and positions much longer than they should have. Some people's poor job performance affected not only me but also other staff members. As a result of dropped balls and others being forced to pick up balls they didn't drop, our church suffered, my life suffered, and our team suffered.

Because I viewed elimination as wrong and allowed certain people to be in certain places much longer than they should have been, our staff lost morale, our church lost momentum, and I lost credibility as a leader. I overestimated the power of training and failed to realize that training helps competence, not character. At the time, I didn't see elimination as an opportunity for both parties to pursue God's next for them.

This can be a reality not only in leadership but also in our relationships. When a dating relationship isn't working out, ending it is a gift you give to both parties involved. There are times when we envision ourselves "hurting" them, but we must reframe it in a way where we see ourselves "releasing" them to pursue God's next and best. We must rethink elimination both personally and professionally. No matter how much it costs to let people go, the price is far greater to let them stay.

We must think of elimination in the realignment of our relationships as *both* a removal and a repositioning. It is a decision we make to remove someone from our relational orbit and to reposition them in a space where they can pursue relationships that are more along the lines of their best interests. Doing this frees us and allows us to create space for relationships that serve our best interests and the purposes of God in our lives.

Once again, if it's prompted by the Spirit, this step is not a matter of selfishness; it's a matter of stewardship. It's a matter of recognizing our responsibility to be a good steward over the life God has given us. Part of stewarding that life, the Scriptures teach, includes guarding our hearts (see Proverbs 4:23) and being a good steward over those to whom we give access to the emotional and relational realms of our lives.

Elimination is also not a matter of convenience; it's a matter of *calling*. In other words, it's not a step we take because we are simply agitated with someone; it's a step we take because we believe it's a necessary step to move into the next chapter of God's story for our life.

CRITERIA FOR ELIMINATION

Elimination should not be made impulsively, arbitrarily, or emotionally. The stakes are too high for us to manage situations like these without establishing some criteria to make these decisions. For me, the criterion for elimination is quite simple. It is when maintaining the relationship, in any form or category, is no longer in the best interests of the persons involved. When the relationship becomes counterproductive, emotionally toxic, spiritually regressive, or physically harmful and dangerous, a person has a responsibility to engage in elimination.

There are several examples in Scripture, but one of the most amazing—and often overlooked—is found in Acts 18. Paul is continuing his ministry and encountering trouble along the way.

> After this, Paul left Athens and went to Corinth. There he met a Jew named Aquila, a native of Pontus, who had recently come from Italy with his wife Priscilla, because Claudius had ordered all Jews to leave Rome. Paul went to see them, and because he was a tentmaker as they were, he stayed and worked with them. Every Sabbath he reasoned in the synagogue, trying to persuade Jews and Greeks.
>
> When Silas and Timothy came from Macedonia, Paul devoted himself exclusively to preaching, testifying to the Jews that Jesus was the Messiah. But when they opposed Paul and became abusive, he shook out his clothes in protest and said to them, "Your blood be on your own heads! I am innocent of it. From now on I will go to the Gentiles."
>
> Then Paul left the synagogue and went next door to the house of Titius Justus, a worshiper of God. Crispus, the

synagogue leader, and his entire household believed in the Lord; and many of the Corinthians who heard Paul believed and were baptized.

Acts 18:1–8

Here we see Paul engaging some Jews in a conversation about Jesus. He's attempting to convince them that Jesus was the promised Messiah. However, in verse 6, the Jews not only opposed Paul, but they became abusive. As soon as that happened, the Scriptures say that Paul shook out his clothes in protest of their actions and said, "Your blood be on your own heads! I am innocent of it. From now on I will go to the Gentiles." Paul was essentially saying, "I'm clear of my responsibility." He then left the synagogue and went to the house of Titius Justus, who was receptive, and it led to many becoming followers of Jesus.

So let's break this down. The language the NIV uses reveals that when the people became abusive, Paul knew it was time for elimination. He was clear that his love for the Jews he was trying to reach did not cancel out God's love for him. Because of this, Paul knew that God was not requesting, requiring, or expecting him to subject himself to abuse for people he loved. Because Paul understood the kind of love that God had for him, he was clear on this also.

Please know that abuse isn't always physical. A person can be in the context of a church where the abuse can be of a spiritual nature—where spiritual authority is confused with control. Allow me to elaborate. In my estimation, a spiritual covering is the equivalent of being an umbrella that provides wisdom and guidance that keeps a person from being exposed to unnecessary elements of life. However, if this relationship becomes abusive, it mutates into becoming a lid, something that limits, restricts, controls, and diminishes. In instances like this, elimination is almost always necessary.

I've been very fortunate and blessed where I've always had kind, loving, and honoring spiritual leadership. However, I know that is not everyone's experience, and there are times when those in different types of circumstances have to make some very difficult decisions.

The same goes for work environments. When a person is being dehumanized, devalued, or disrespected, and you clearly see that the relationship is working in direct opposition to what God is attempting to do in and through your life, it's time to consider elimination. In fact, all of these scenarios align with the criteria of elimination. When setting limitations does not protect you, when realignment and repositioning don't serve you, it's time to think through elimination.

THE RISKS OF ELIMINATION

Elimination is risky, right?

Sure. Mostly because it's absolutely important to be accurate in your assessment before eliminating a relationship. Remember earlier when I talked about the different disciples of Jesus—one named Peter and one named Judas. Both of them engaged in what some people would call betrayal. Peter denied his affiliation and association with Jesus three times. Judas actually sold Jesus out for money. Both people betrayed Jesus. But the key difference shows the discernment of Jesus. One of these men had a bad heart, a deeply selfish motive, and the other had a bad day and a very human fear of being killed. If Peter would have been completely eliminated from Jesus' life, then we would have lost a key and consequential figure in the New Testament.

So the risk in the elimination consideration is that we can confuse a Peter with a Judas. We may find ourselves eliminating someone who is having a bad day, week, or month and not someone who truly has a bad heart and evil intentions.

Another risk is that we can sometimes find ourselves eliminating people correctly who are also individuals who add some value to our lives. This can be especially true in work environments. There are times when we may have an employee whose skill set and competence bring great value to the company, but their attitude does great damage to the culture. The negativity they're bringing to the work environment is far outweighing the benefits their gift brings. And yet that doesn't change the fact that their gift is valuable. There will be some kind of loss if that person no longer works there.

At the end of the day, be aware of the risks, but don't allow the risks to be a deterrent when you know in your heart of hearts that you must eliminate someone from your life.

HOW TO ELIMINATE SOMEONE FROM OUR LIVES . . . IN LOVE

The process for eliminating someone from our lives safely and with the most love should happen in three steps—in three Ps.

PRAY

First of all, **pray**. Prayer is incredibly important. And I'm not just saying this as a pastor. It's not just a churchy phrase or religious rhetoric. It is a key and practical part of the process.

Prayer is going to sober us emotionally. Everyone can make a decision, but decisions are like cars—something is always driving them. We want to make sure that when we make a decision to eliminate a relationship, our emotions are not at the wheel of the car. They will likely be *in* the car. Emotions do have some influence on the decisions we make. But those emotions should only be passengers. They should not be driving the car. The emotional sobriety that comes from prayer is a way to counter our tendencies to operate from a hurt and wounded place, where we will be prone to misinterpret things in our relationships and act impulsively. We must allow prayer to center us so we act with empathy, no matter what we decide.

Prayer also keeps us on a God-honoring course when dealing with the person we intend to eliminate from our lives. Even when someone does us wrong, we still have an obligation to treat them right. Remember the Golden Rule? There is a way to remove someone from our lives that is a reflection of how we would want to be treated if the tables were turned. We should ask ourselves, *If someone were to eliminate me, how would I want them to treat me? What would I want them to say to me? How would I want them to manage my responses?* Prayer centers you so you can enact this decision in the best possible way, relative to the person you are talking to. There is, of course, no universal approach and no formulas. Be led by the Spirit, and you have the best shot of doing this right.

That's something else that prayer offers us. We all need inner guidance on the best way to do a hard thing. We all should want to find the most sensitive way to do this challenging thing. Praying reveals that we are open to allowing the Spirit of God to give us guidance.

Bottom line? Think of prayer as an adjustment for our eyes. We've got two eyes in our heads that give us sight, but we've also got the eyes of our hearts that give us vision. The eyes in our hearts help us see beyond what we see in the natural. We see something with *these* eyes and we can't pick wrong.

Prayer helps us see first of all what we need and not just what we like. Too many of us pick people to be in our circle that we like as opposed to people we need. The hard truth is that sometimes people who are called to be assets in our lives are going to have some things about them that are agitating. Don't be the person who loses an asset because you can't handle a little agitation.

PLAN

After prayer, there must be a **plan**. One of the biggest issues that can come up in a conversation involving removal and elimination is the question of timing. When is the best time to enact this decision? Elimination conversations should be ad hoc conversations. If we're saying things too quickly, we may be saying them from an emotional place. If we're speaking emotionally, we may be speaking irrationally and insensitively. Again, it's not wrong to be emotional or to allow emotion to be a part of a conversation, but our emotions can't be leading the decision. It's not safe for our emotions to drive this car. When we turn over the wheel to our emotions, it's entirely possible we will find ourselves doing the right thing at the wrong time.

We need to consider several things when planning an elimination conversation:

- When am I going to have this conversation?
- Where?
- What is the best space?
- Will this conversation evoke some emotion in them that will cause them to be embarrassed if expressed publicly?
- If so, where am I going to do this?
- What words will I use in order to make sure I clearly and concisely convey my point?

The Scriptures say that a conversation should be seasoned with grace (see Colossians 4:6). It's important to remember that grace is a gift given to those who don't deserve it. It is favor we don't earn. So it is necessary to demonstrate grace to people who have injured us and who, consequently, we may have to eliminate from our lives. The greatest expression of this is Jesus, who as he hung on a cross asked the Father to forgive his perpetrators because they didn't know what they were doing (see Luke 23:34).

| PERFORM

The final *P* is **perform**. Relationships don't change because of intention; they change because of execution. A person can pray and plan, but at some point, they have to perform. One of the key catalysts is courage. Consider Joshua as he assumed leadership responsibilities for the Hebrew people. In Joshua 1, we see him transitioning as Moses' successor, and God is giving him a pep talk of sorts before he steps into the role.

> After the death of Moses the servant of the LORD, the LORD said to Joshua son of Nun, Moses' aide: "Moses my servant is dead. Now then, you and all these people, get ready to cross the Jordan River into the land I am about to give to them—to the Israelites. I will give you every place where you set your foot, as I promised Moses. Your territory will extend from the desert to Lebanon, and from the great river, the Euphrates—all the Hittite country—to the Mediterranean Sea in the west. No one will be able to stand against you all the days of your life. As I was with Moses, so I will be with you; I will never leave you nor forsake you. Be strong and courageous, because you will lead these people to inherit the land I swore to their ancestors to give them."
>
> *Joshua 1:1–6*

God is communicating with Joshua very clearly here. He is essentially saying to him, "Now, listen. You're about to move forward into some activity. As I was with Moses, I will be with you. This is what you need to do most in this season: Be strong and have courage." God didn't tell Joshua to *feel* strong and *feel* courageous; he told him to *act* courageously.

It would be disingenuous of me to say that our elimination conversations won't produce conflicting emotions. There may certainly be fear, trepidation, guilt, and maybe even shame. But we must *act* courageously, despite what we feel in that moment. Courage, we know, is not the elimination of fear; it is acting in spite of fear. Courage is allowing a superior fear to drive your decisions as opposed to being imprisoned by an inferior fear.

An inferior fear looks like this: *I'm afraid of what will happen if I do this.* A superior fear looks like this: *I'm afraid of what will happen if I don't do this.* When the rubber meets the road, there must be execution. Courage gives us the ability to do exactly that.

SELF-ELIMINATION AND EXTERNAL ELIMINATION

I use self-elimination to refer to the choice a person makes to eliminate themselves from a relationship without an elimination discussion. There are times when a relationship is not working out because of *our* inability to fulfill the role we've been assigned in that person's life. And as a result, we eliminate ourselves from the relationship before the person comes to share why they are eliminating us. If you've ever done this or this has ever happened to you—a person has simply disappeared from your life—then you know that this can sometimes be an answer to prayer. The person valued us enough to make the elimination decision for us.

External elimination happens when seasons and circumstances beyond our control contribute to the elimination of a relationship. Maybe a friend moves to another part of the country, and communication dwindles. Sometimes a single person gets married, and that affects the dynamics of the person's relationships with other single people. Whatever form elimination takes in our lives, it is incredibly important to enter that decision with humility and the willingness to demonstrate the grace that God has freely extended to us.

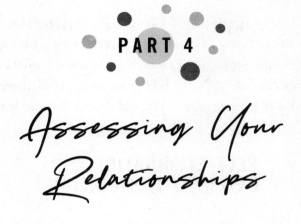

PART 4

Assessing Your Relationships

So we have everyone in the right places in our lives—do they stay there forever? Not likely. It's important to periodically evaluate and assess the relationships we have, as well as our own behaviors and participation in these partnerships. It's also vital that all parties understand the significance of *being* a good friend, even as we seek to have good friends. The Bible says, "A man who has friends must himself be friendly" (Proverbs 18:24 NKJV). As much as we need to assess the people in our lives, we also need to assess ourselves to ensure that we are being the very person we desire to attract.

WHAT KIND OF FRIEND ARE YOU?

In all our talk about categories and alignment, we must consider the roles *we* play in the health of our relationships. We must ask, particularly as it relates to the friend category, "What kind of friend am I?"

There are three types of friends we can be. We can be the friend we'd like to be, the friend others want us to be, or the friend God needs us to be. Spoiler alert! Those three don't always line up. As a result, we need to regularly assess where we are in a relationship and be willing to evaluate our own actions. The ability to make honest and accurate assessments of our own engagements in relationship is an important life skill. It determines how wise our decisions are going to be and whether or not we or the people we are in relationships with are able to correct a behavior in order to have full and fulfilling interactions. It is the essence of relational intelligence.

Most of the assessments we do are outward. That has been the focus of this book thus far. We are assessing others and determining what kind of friends we actually want. This is 100 percent okay to do. External assessment isn't evil. As I've noted many times, it is one of the most important things we can do to make sure we are stewarding our lives properly. It's what we must do if we want our lives to be a gift that adds value to the lives of others.

However, I think living with relational intelligence isn't just about assessing other relationships; it's also about assessing ourselves. Andy Stanley, in a message on singleness, posed this self-reflective question: "Are you who the person you are looking for is looking for?"[21]

APPLIES ACROSS THE BOARD

We often think self-assessment is more significant in romantic relationships. I would submit that it is necessary in *all* relationships. A person in a business relationship should ask themselves, *Am I the coworker that the coworker I'm looking for is looking for? Am I the supervisor that the person I want to supervise is looking for?* Every year, I host a one-day personal development event called "Thrive," where business and religious leaders from all over the country come for a day of personal development in Orlando. Most recently, we were discussing this idea of team building and how to build a great team and attract great people. The discussion ultimately led to some powerful revelations.

Everyone wants a great team, and everyone wants a team filled with stars. We all want to work with people who are capable and competent. One of the things that surprised those who took part in our discussion was my assertion that it's hard to get great people to want to work with and for you if you don't become the kind of leader great people want to work with and work for.

I've experienced this personally. At one point in my pastoral ministry, I was really praying and hoping that God would surround me with a staff that was very competent and capable of taking our organization to the next level. Up until that point, I had been very fortunate for the most part to have an incredible team. But during this particular season, I felt like we needed a little something extra. As I was considering the type of people I was praying for, I had to ask myself a very difficult question: *Am I the type of leader they would want to follow—the type of leader who could actually lead them?* I had to ask myself if I was the person the people I was looking for were looking for. A self-assessment was absolutely necessary in order to position myself for the blessing of something "extra."

And so it goes with all of our relationships.

In every sphere of relationships, this principle applies. It's especially true in friendships. Again, we must continuously ask ourselves, *Am I the type of person that the type of person I'm looking for is looking for?* The Bible puts it this way: "A man who has friends must himself be friendly" (Proverbs 18:24 NKJV). Self-assessment is important because the type of person you are will be an indication of the type of people you draw to your life.

To be clear, it doesn't mean you're going to draw the same type of people into your life. A selfish person doesn't always draw a selfish person into his or her life. But if a nonselfish person stays in a relationship with a selfish person, it may mean they are super needy with low esteem. Or they may have some other trait that will be either fulfilled by the selfish person or ignored (which, of course, will only amplify their neediness). There is likely some emotional unhealthiness that is allowing them to be in a relationship that's lopsided and one-sided.

Likewise, a generous person may not always draw a person who is generous. To stay in relationship with that person, though, they may have some other trait, some other broken-ness that is filled or ignored by the nongenerous person. Again, this is the way they can stay in a relationship where there's no reciprocity.

People stay in unhealthy relationships all the time. The relational side of our lives also seems to be the part where we can be well-intentioned but use our brain the least. This is where the act of doing regular self-assessment is critical. It helps us see where we may or may not be a gift in another person's life. That's really what purpose is all about. Purpose is the reason for the creation or existence of a thing. We were created for more than ourselves.

SELF-ASSESSMENT MAKES US BETTER FOR OTHERS

We were created for more than self-pleasure. We were created for more than our own happiness. The truth of the matter is that people who live their lives in pursuit of only pleasure and happiness usually find that it always eludes them. You'll never find fulfillment until you find your purpose, and your purpose is going to be found making unique contributions to the lives of others. So *being* a certain kind of friend, as opposed to just *having* certain kinds of friends, is going to bring you great fulfillment.

Remember when I said there are three types of friends we can be: the friend we'd like to be, the friend others want us to be, and the friend God needs us to be? Well, let's do a deep dive into each of these.

THE FRIEND WE'D LIKE TO BE

Sometimes the friend we'd like to be may not be the friend others want us to be. Sometimes the friend others want us to be is not the friend that God needs us to be. As I discussed early on in the book, friendship is God's idea. And yet, when it comes to the friend we want to be, most of us give in friendship what we want in one. We are generous in the areas of friendship where we want people to be generous with us.

We give what comes easily or naturally for us. If we love support, we'll give support. If we love affirmation, we'll give affirmation. But just because we're giving to a friend, just because we're being the kind of friend we want, does not mean we're actually meeting the greatest area of need in the lives of our friends. If I'm providing support because that's the friend I want to be—the supportive friend—but I'm not telling the truth, then I'm the friend I want to be but I'm not the friend God needs me to be. And that can be deeply problematic and will likely end up in a realignment of the relationship by either party.

THE FRIEND OTHERS WANT US TO BE

We all have different expectations of what it actually means to be a friend, and there are times when people are going to need difficult things from us as a friend. This is the second type of friend we can be—the kind that others need—and it's not something we should shun or not consider. What we must do, though, is something that one of my mentors, Chris Hodges, says often. We should consider what people *want* from us but always give them what they *need*.

There are times when people will want things from us that are not in either of our best interests. There are times when people will want things from us that require us to cross boundaries we don't need to cross. People will sometimes want things from us that require us to engage in activities that aren't necessarily healthy for us, or they will want something we're convinced is not good for them.

The story of Joab and King David applies perfectly here. If we look closely at 2 Samuel 11, we see these dynamics play out in textbook fashion.

David had sent Joab and the Israelite army off to war, and David stayed back. While he was in Jerusalem, he saw from his palace roof a woman bathing and sent messengers to find her and bring her to him. So while this king should have been with his army, he instead slept with a woman who was not his wife. Soon after, she sends him a message saying she is pregnant. And David immediately responded.

So David sent this word to Joab: "Send me Uriah the Hittite." And Joab sent him to David. When Uriah came to him, David asked him how Joab was, how the soldiers were and how the war was going. Then David said to Uriah, "Go down to your house and wash your feet." So Uriah left the palace, and a gift from the king was sent after him. But Uriah slept at the entrance to the palace with all his master's servants and did not go down to his house.

David was told, "Uriah did not go home." So he asked Uriah, "Haven't you just come from a military campaign? Why didn't you go home?"

2 Samuel 11:6–10

Uriah told David he could not possibly think of feasting and relaxing with his wife at home while his comrades were still vulnerably camped near the enemy. So David tried again, inviting Uriah to dine with him and making sure he had too much to drink so he'd go home to his wife for certain this time. But Uriah would not.

In the morning David wrote a letter to Joab and sent it with Uriah. In it he wrote, "Put Uriah out in front where the fighting is fiercest. Then withdraw from him so he will be struck down and die."

So while Joab had the city under siege, he put Uriah at a place where he knew the strongest defenders were. When the men of the city came out and fought against Joab, some of the men in David's army fell; moreover, Uriah the Hittite died . . .

When Uriah's wife heard that her husband was dead, she mourned for him. After the time of mourning was over,

David had her brought to his house, and she became his wife and bore him a son. But the thing David had done displeased the LORD.

2 Samuel 11:14–17, 26–27

| THE FRIEND GOD NEEDS US TO BE

In summary, Joab was the friend that David wanted him to be but not the friend God needed him to be. He gave David what he wanted—he killed Uriah so David could have Uriah's wife, Bathsheba—but it wasn't what God needed. Our friends do not need us to be someone who aids and assists them in destroying their lives. They do not need someone who remains silent when speaking the truth is necessary.

Too often, there's an expectation that because we're friends, I'm supposed to be silent. That inevitably ends in disaster. Consider Adam and Eve in the book of Genesis. We know the story, right?

Now the serpent was more crafty than any of the wild animals the LORD God had made. He said to the woman, "Did God really say, 'You must not eat from any tree in the garden'?"

The woman said to the serpent, "We may eat fruit from the trees in the garden, but God did say, 'You must not eat fruit from the tree that is in the middle of the garden, and you must not touch it, or you will die.'"

"You will not certainly die," the serpent said to the woman. "For God knows that when you eat from it your eyes will be opened, and you will be like God, knowing good and evil."

Genesis 3:1–5

So Adam and Eve are successfully coerced by the serpent to eat the forbidden fruit. Too often when the story is told, it's told in a way that suggests Eve was by herself and Adam was somewhere else playing with animals. But the text says that Adam was with her. Adam was present when Eve ate, but he was also silent. This is the first relationship breach because God did not design relationships to work that way. What if Adam would have spoken up? How different would the world be? Instead of choosing to not be silent when it mattered most, he assisted someone in doing what was not best for them.

Don't be Adam.

The friend God needs you to be is the friend your friend actually needs. And what do they need? They need truth. They need a person who considers their wants but is committed to their needs. A person who has an accurate understanding of what godly love is, which is not a feeling. Godly love, called *agape* in the Greek, is an incomparable benevolence. It is a commitment to always do what is in the best interest of that person. Godly love is loving the person even more than the relationship. When we can say, "I love you so much I'm willing to lose the relationship if it means I take a stand for what I know is best for you," that's when we know we are being the right kind of friend.

A MODEL FOR HEALTHY RELATIONSHIP BUILDING

It's incredibly important to me to have biblical models for some of the concepts I've covered in this book. In the biblical text, I find numerous demonstrations of how relationships should or should not play out. In Romans 15:4, the apostle Paul writes, "For everything that was written in the past was written to teach us, so that through the endurance taught in the Scriptures and the encouragement they provide we might have hope."

So when we examine the lives of certain individuals in Scripture, their lives can be instruments of education for us. Their stories aren't there just so we can look at them and talk about them. They exist in our sacred text so we can learn from them. An incredible example of the importance of becoming the kind of person you want in your life is found in the story of Ruth.

RUTH'S RELATIONSHIPS

Now Elimelek, Naomi's husband, died, and she was left with her two sons. They married Moabite women, one named Orpah and the other Ruth. After they had lived there about ten years, both Mahlon and Kilion also died, and Naomi was left without her two sons and her husband.

When Naomi heard in Moab that the LORD had come to the aid of his people by providing food for them, she and her daughters-in-law prepared to return home from there. With her two daughters-in-law she left the place where she had been living and set out on the road that would take them back to the land of Judah.

Then Naomi said to her two daughters-in-law, "Go back, each of you, to your mother's home. May the LORD show you kindness, as you have shown kindness to your dead husbands and to me. May the LORD grant that each of you will find rest in the home of another husband."

Then she kissed them goodbye and they wept aloud and said to her, "We will go back with you to your people."

But Naomi said, "Return home, my daughters. Why would you come with me? Am I going to have any more sons, who could become your husbands? Return home, my daughters; I am too old to have another husband. Even if I thought there was still hope for me—even if I had a husband tonight and then gave birth to sons— would you wait until they grew up? Would you remain unmarried for them? No, my daughters. It is more bitter for me than for you, because the LORD's hand has turned against me!"

At this they wept aloud again. Then Orpah kissed her mother-in-law goodbye, but Ruth clung to her.

Ruth 1:3–14

We see a few critical relationships in Ruth's orbit, even though, if I'm honest, the categories that show up in Ruth's life are not exactly clear. The first one is with her mother-in-law, Naomi. We can certainly see Naomi as an advisor. Some may even argue that there is a friendship component—at the very least, a spirit of friendship—between the two. Ruth and her sister-in-law, Orpah, married two brothers. Orpah could be viewed as an associate, particularly in light of the distance between them that would occur later. And over the course of their relationship, we can assume that Boaz, whom Ruth meets later, became Ruth's friend. That said, the dynamics and interactions of these individuals are still great models for how we do relationships.

As Scripture above notes, Naomi's husband and her two sons die, leaving all three women widowed. When this happens, Naomi encourages her daughters-in-law to go back to their homeland. She is grieving and bitter and recognizes that it will probably be in their best interest to go back so they can remarry.

In those days, it was really difficult for women to fend for themselves, by themselves. Naomi recognized this, despite being deeply traumatized. She was selfless enough to encourage Ruth and Orpah to make decisions that were in their best interest. She could have thought about her own loneliness, her own desire for companionship. She could have asked them to stay, but she didn't.

Orpah took Naomi up on her offer and went back to her homeland. And despite what you might have been taught—Orpah gets a bad rap sometimes in sermons—this wasn't necessarily an inappropriate decision. It was simply her decision, her path. Leaving wasn't disloyal because Naomi had made it clear that leaving was in their best interest. Orpah chose that route and understood that she alone was responsible for executing the decision that was in her best interest. God gave us the gift of choice, and our lives are going to be a reflection of what we do with that gift.

That said, Ruth decided to make a different choice. She chose not to go back to her homeland. She said to Naomi, "Wherever you go I'm going. Your people are going to be my people. Your God is going to be my God" (Ruth 1:16, my paraphrase). So Naomi went back to her homeland, and Ruth went with her.

Now, Ruth's decision to stay with Naomi is also a reflection of a person who's making a decision *not* to act *solely* in their own interest. In fact, Caitlyn Anderson in "3 Lessons on Friendship" says that the relationship between Naomi and Ruth is so powerful that it has an even larger takeaway:

> It's no secret that our world is very divided right now. We, as a society, tend to "stick to our own"—which means that the boundaries of age, race, religion, etc. are very much still there. If we were all to follow the example of Ruth and Naomi when it comes to befriending those different than us, we could change the world overnight. Not only is embracing difference necessary to live together, but it also helps us build wholesome communities.[22]

Whatever the case, Ruth is living outside of herself and demonstrating loyalty and support. She is committed to Naomi, not for what she can get from her, but for who she is. Again, this is the essence of friendship.

After a series of events, Ruth ended up meeting a wealthy, influential individual named Boaz. From there we get this incredible love story that has been taught across the ages. In the church context, Ruth and Boaz's relationship has become the ideal for men and women. People who see themselves in the position of Ruth want a Boaz, and people who see themselves in the position of Boaz want a Ruth.

And while there are certainly romantic implications, I'd like to explore this relationship from a different perspective. There is so much to learn relationally here. Ruth wanted a secure, successful, sensitive, God-fearing man, and Boaz wanted a loving, kind, generous, strong, resilient, nonexploitive, non-deceptive woman. But the truth that's often overlooked is this: In order to get a Boaz, you have to become a Ruth. In order to get a Ruth, you have to become a Boaz.

Many, if not most, of us don't always think about whether we have become the kind of person we need to be in order to pull the relationships we need into our life. Boaz had wealth and influence, and he ended up in a relationship with a person who would not exploit his wealth and influence. Ruth was strong. She was resilient. And she ended up in a relationship with someone who wasn't intimidated by her strength (see Ruth 3). Who they each were separately set the stage for what the relationship would ultimately be.

Are you the kind of person who can handle strength? Are you intimidated by it? Does it upset you? Consider your answers when wondering why you may or may not draw people into your life who demonstrate strength. This is true of other traits as well. If we find ourselves saying, *I want people in my life who will tell me the truth*, then the question is, *Are we becoming the kind of person who can handle the truth?* If we say, *I want people in my life who will help me carry out my dreams,* we must ask, *Am I the kind of person who is willing to share power?* If we say, *I want the kind of person who's going to be there for me when I need them,* then the question is, *Are we the kind of person who people want to be there for?*

It's interesting that we would explore Ruth as a model for how relationships show up, because many generations later, one of her descendants would be our ultimate model for the alignment and management of relationships. Jesus had an advisor in the heavenly Father, and he had people, like the Samaritan woman (see John 4), who were called to him as assignments. He had people who followed his ministry closely, called the Seventy, who were associates, as well as, of course, the Three and the Twelve we discussed earlier.

Jesus is a wonderful model for managing relationships and the inspiration for this book. And Ruth is a great example as well of what it means to become the kind of person you need to become in order to get the kind of relationships you desire.

HOW'S IT GOING?

It's one thing to share the various categories of relationships and how to align people properly in our lives; it's another to offer tools for us to evaluate both ourselves and our relationships. That's what I'd like to do here—check in to see how we are applying what we've learned in the book. Remember, the goal here is not perfect relationships but an awareness, a consciousness even, of what's required of us and others in order to have healthy engagements with the people God brings into our lives.

WHY ASSESSMENT, AGAIN?

The goal of the assessment is twofold. First, *assessment is for you; it's for me.* Jesus says, "Until I take the plank out of my own eye, I cannot clearly see the splinter in my brother's" (Matthew 7:5, my paraphrase). He is making the assertion that without dealing with our own issues first, our ability to accurately assess what's going on with other people is going to be impaired. We are removing "the plank" out of our own eyes so we will be able to see things more accurately and clearly in our second assessment—the assessment we make of our relationships.

This shows up in our relationship intelligence equation also. The EQ in the EQ + IQ = RQ is about self-awareness. Whatever you're looking for in your life—a friend, an associate, an assignment, or an advisor—you will probably end up being in someone else's life. A great example of this is if you're a parent, you're an advisor. This is inherent in the role.

So the first assessment is a self-evaluation questionnaire designed to identify *who we are* in our relationships.

Personal Assessment

FRIEND

In what ways do I demonstrate unshakable character in my friendships?

Am I known for my unconditional love?

How honest am I with my friends? Do I tell the truth in love?

What level of reliability have I shown in my friendships?

ASSOCIATE

Am I considered trustworthy by those I work with or employ?

How do I handle distance in the relationship? Am I fine with very little communication, or do I desire more from a particular individual?

ASSIGNMENT

Am I humble? How so, or why not?

Am I teachable? How so, or why not?

Am I available? Why, or why not?

ADVISOR

Am I capable of teaching discipline and self-restraint?

How's It Going?

Do I have the ability to invest time and resources into an individual?

Have I accomplished enough professionally, personally, and/or spiritually to pour into someone else?

Our second assessment is a relational intelligence tool designed to evaluate our relationships and where we've placed them in our lives.

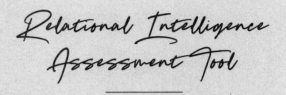

Relational Intelligence Assessment Tool

Part One: Identification

In this assessment, you will examine the people in your relational circle. Most of our relationship circles start off as a pot of gumbo. Everyone is mixed up and misaligned. This tool will help you evaluate all the relationships in your life and see, based on what you've read, if you've got the right people in the right places. After filling out the first chart, ask yourself, *Do I have someone in the friends box who should be in the associates box? Do I have someone in the associates box who should be in the assignments box? Do I have someone in the friends box who should be in the advisors box?*

Take a moment to list the names of individuals under the categories that reflect where they currently exist in your life.

Utilizing the questions presented in each corresponding chapter, pray about and evaluate each name. Place a check mark (☑) by a name that's listed in the proper category. Place an *M* (for "move") by a name that, based on your reflection and evaluation, you may need to move to another category. Write in your journal about the impact of this transition on your heart and on other relationships. On the next page, use the same chart to create a revised relationship map that denotes the transitions and changes.

Friends	Associates

Assignments	Advisors

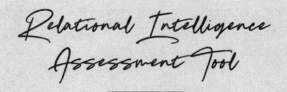

Relational Intelligence Assessment Tool

Part Two: Realignment

Misplaced people produce misplaced expectations, and misplaced expectations always lead to frustration. And frustration ultimately leads to bitterness. Proper alignment is the key to avoiding these unintended consequences of not stewarding relationships well.

In the boxes below, use the changes made in the previous chart to create a new relationship map.

Friends	Associates
Assignments	**Advisors**

Take some time, however much you need, to reflect on and evaluate these changes. Afterward, review the changes and decide what conversations you will need to have and with whom.

Name of person:

Type of conversation (circle): Realignment or Elimination
Planned points:

Name of person:

Type of conversation (circle): Realignment or Elimination
Planned points:

Name of person:

Type of conversation (circle): Realignment or Elimination
Planned points:

Name of person:

Type of conversation (circle): Realignment or Elimination
Planned points:

Use the planned points above and the scripts below to help develop the conversations you must have.

QUESTIONS TO CONSIDER WHEN DISCERNING YOUR RELATIONSHIPS
Reflection
Create a list of quiet places you can go regularly to reflect. This may be your prayer closet at home, the riverfront, or an actual retreat.

Consider writing the answers to your questions in a journal. I also recommend posing these questions a few times at multiple points in a day. You'd be surprised at how much an answer will change or become more detailed over time.

How's It Going?

In the relationship I'm in . . .
What am I feeling? Am I frustrated? Do I feel drained? If so, in what area?

Why am I frustrated?

What am I actually expecting that isn't being met?

What's missing in my life that's needed?

Evaluation (Fruit Inspection)
Where am I in this relationship? (Think about the posture of your heart, mind, and soul.)

What do I need in this relationship? (Be as specific as possible.)

What am I currently getting from this relationship?
(Again, be specific.)

What do I need to do to obtain what I need from this relationship?
(Think: actual actions.)

SCRIPTS AND QUESTIONS FOR ALIGNING YOUR RELATIONSHIPS

It's important to note that these scripts were not created to be a "one size fits all" way to approach the conversations you'll need to have with people in your life whose roles need adjusting. These are simply designed to offer a framework and the language needed to accomplish an adjustment that will serve both parties in the long run. The scripts are only guides, so please feel free to rework and rephrase as you feel led.

Scripts for Realignment

Relationships that are moving from intimate to distant
(for example, friend to associate, advisor to associate)

"I greatly value our relationship and the contributions you've made to my life. You're one of the most significant and important people in my life. You've probably noticed over the past couple of months or so that things have been different with me. There are some things I've been thinking through and reassessing in my own life. I am recalibrating and refocusing for the future. As a result, I feel like I must make some adjustments in my relationships right now."

"I've been throwing myself so much into my career [or family]. I've been trying to spend some time developing myself and doing some self-improvement. Because of that work, I've had to shift the way I relate to you and the nature of our relationship. I wanted you to be aware of that. I wanted you to know that as I sort through this, my time is going to be limited. I won't be able to spend as much time doing some of the things we used to do. I would really appreciate just your love and your understanding and your support as I work through this. I value you. I love you. And I greatly need you to continue to be a part of my life in some way. I really need your support as I sort through what life looks like for me in this next season."

Relationships that are moving from distant to more intimate
(for example, associate to friend, associate to advisor)

"We've been working together for [whatever number of] years. I've had the opportunity to get to know you, and I feel like you're an incredible person. You're trustworthy, kind, etc. I'm kind of in a season in my life where I've been looking for friendships. I don't want to make any assumptions about the way you view our relationship, but I do want you to know that I see you that way and I would love to cultivate and develop a friendship with someone like you."

"I think we've moved past the point of me pouring my expertise out for your own personal development. You've shown yourself to be a person who is trustworthy and genuine, and I feel like it would bring me great joy to have you in my life as a friend. I don't know where you are in life, what all you have going on. But I did want to communicate what I felt, just in case you felt the same thing and would be open to that. I would love to continue pursuing a friendship with you."

"I've watched you from afar. I've learned so much from watching you. I know someone like you is incredibly busy and has great demands on you. But I would be honored and fortunate if in some way you could serve as an advisor or mentor in my life. We can discuss what that looks like for you. I'm open to different forms."

"If I'm honest, what I've seen in you—your example, competence, exposure, and capabilities—is something that could probably save me years. It could help me tremendously. I would truly be honored if you would consider exploring the possibility of developing a mentoring relationship with me. I'm flexible enough to be open to the different ways that something like this has to flesh itself out. But I would really love to have you in that space in my life."

Scripts for Boundary Setting

"I'm in a season in my life when I might share certain personal aspects of my life. If I feel like those things need to be maintained in a safe space, I want to have the comfort in knowing that this has taken place. And I feel like the last couple of things I've shared with you, for whatever reason, have not been held in the kind of confidence I need. So because of that, I have to make some adjustments in our relationship for my own sanity and peace of mind."

"One of the things that's really important to me right now is my own emotional health, having my own space and the ability to focus on my life. I want to have a positive perspective on life because it's way too easy to beat up on myself and my family for my work. I want you to know, though, that it's really hard to do these things if I feel like I'm in an environment where I'm constantly being talked down to and insulted. There are times when you and I engage in a conversation, I feel I could be potentially talked down to. I've had a couple of conversations with you before about how the way you communicate makes me feel, and now I just want to let you know that I have to make adjustments in our relationship before that takes place again. If you begin to become abusive or combative in a way that is uncomfortable for me, I'm going to have to remove myself from the room. I'm not attempting to be disrespectful. I'm not attempting to be dishonorable. What I am attempting to do is preserve my own sense of mental stability and health."

Scripts prior to Elimination

Before diving into the scripts for elimination, you'll need to ask yourself a few questions.

When am I going to have this conversation?

Will this conversation evoke some emotion in them that will cause them to be embarrassed if expressed publicly? Which emotions are possible?

If so, where am I going to do this?

What words will I use to make sure I clearly and concisely convey my point?

Scripts for Elimination

"One of the things that's really important to me right now is my own emotional health. It's crucial that I have a positive perspective on life because it's way too easy to allow outside influences to affect my heart, mind, and soul. It can be challenging to do this when there is constant and never-ending conflict. I'm not afraid of conflict in my relationships, but at some point, I have to take inventory of how those conflicts affect my mental and emotional state. Right now, I need some time to do that kind of inventory, and that is going to mean I will need to put some space between us."

"You have been such an important part of my development as a person, and I'm not dismissing that. I am very grateful for your contribution to me. I'm just asking that right now you understand I need a little time and space."

QUESTIONS FOR SELF-ASSESSMENT

List ten of your most prominent character traits (consider the ones that people say about you the most—positive and constructive). For example, "You are always on time." "You have a short fuse."

Think about the character traits of the person whose role you are considering adjusting in your life or the person you are looking to add to your life. List at least ten below.

Make note of where the traits listed above for you both are complimentary and where they diverge.

In light of this information, are you who the person you are looking for is looking for?

Take a moment to pray over what you've written. Ask God to give you guidance and direction.

A follow-up question: Are you who the person in your life needs, according to God's will and purpose for their life?

ACKNOWLEDGMENTS

My executive coach once told me you don't go as far as your dream; you go as far as your team. This axiom is gospel truth. This book is a team effort and the result of a collaboration of gifts, energy, and effort from an amazing group of people.

I want to begin by acknowledging the incredible team at Change Church. They are more than teammates; they are family.

I also want to thank the outstanding team at Dupree Miller, who have been nothing short of amazing.

I also want to acknowledge Zondervan, who believed in this book, championed it, and fought to get it in the hands of as many people as possible.

I also want to thank Marc Jeffrey and Legacy Consulting Group, who believed in me in ways I didn't believe in myself. Thank you for your partnership in life and ministry.

Finally, to every friend, associate, assignment, and advisor— thank you; you are by far some of God's greatest gifts to me.

NOTES

1. See Jim Collins, *Good to Great: Why Some Companies Make the Leap . . . and Others Don't* (New York: HarperBusiness, 2001), 13.
2. P. Salovey and J. D. Mayer, "Emotional Intelligence," *Imagination, Cognition, and Personality* 9, no. 3 (1990): 185–211.
3. Brené Brown, *The Gifts of Imperfection: Let Go of Who You Think You're Supposed to Be and Embrace Who You Are* (Center City, MN: Hazelden, 2010), 56.
4. Van Moody, *The People Factor: How Building Great Relationships and Ending Bad Ones Unlocks Your God-Given Purpose* (Nashville: Nelson, 2014), xiv.
5. Henri Nouwen, *Out of Solitude: Three Meditations on the Christian Life* (Notre Dame, IN: Ave Marie, 1974), 34.
6. Gary Chapman, *The 5 Love Languages: The Secret to Love That Lasts* (1992; repr., Chicago: Northfield, 2010).
7. Stephen R. Covey, *Primary Greatness: The 12 Levers of Success* (New York: Simon & Schuster, 2015), 80.
8. Drs. Henry Cloud and John Townsend, *Boundaries: When to Say Yes, How to Say No, to Take Control of Your Life* (1992; repr., Grand Rapids: Zondervan, 2017), 34.
9. See Stephen H. Covey, *The Seven Habits of Highly Effective People: Powerful Lessons in Personal Change* (1989; repr., New York: Free Press, 2004), 94–144.
10. Dan B. Allender and Tremper Longman III, *The Cry of the Soul: How Our Emotions Reveal Our Deepest Questions About God* (Colorado Springs: NavPress, 2015), 14.

11. Susan David and Christina Congleton, "Emotional Agility," *Harvard Business Review* (November 2013), https://hbr.org/2013/11/emotional-agility.

12. Henry Cloud, *Never Go Back: 10 Things You'll Never Do Again* (New York: Howard, 2014), 24.

13. Cited in "One of Dr. Maya Angelou's Most Important Lessons," Book Club Finale, *The Oprah Winfrey Show*, June 18, 1997, www.oprah.com/own-oprahshow/one-of-dr-maya-angelous-most-important-lessons_1.

14. See Dr. Henry Cloud, *Boundaries for Leaders: Results, Relationships, and Being Ridiculously in Charge* (New York: HarperBusiness, 2013).

15. Dharius Daniels, *Represent Jesus: Rethink Your Version of Christianity and Become More Like Christ* (Lake Mary, FL: Charisma Media, 2014).

16. Cited in Erin Gabriel, "Understanding Emotional Intelligence and Its Effect on Your Life," CNN Health, July 26, 2018, www.cnn.com/2018/04/11/health/improve-emotional-intelligence/index.html.

17. Quoted in Gabriel, "Understanding Emotional Intelligence."

18. Lisa Quast, "4 Tips for Finding Great Career Mentors," *Forbes*, January 2, 2013, www.forbes.com/sites/lisaquast/2013/01/02/4-tips-for-finding-great-career-mentors/#6a5a1b77f2ff.

19. Cloud and Townsend, *Boundaries*, 31, 33, 45, 47, italics original.

20. Becky Sweat, "Six Characteristics of Biblical Friendship," *Discern* (September/October 2018), https://lifehopeandtruth.com/relationships/friendship/six-characteristics-of-biblical-friendship.

21. Quoted in Eryn Sun, "Andy Stanley Dispels the 'Right Person' Myth," *Christian Post*, May 3, 2011, www.christianpost.com/news/andy-stanley-dispels-the-right-person-myth.html.

22. Caitlyn Anderson, "3 Lessons on Friendship from Ruth & Naomi," Everyday Ediths, August 24, 2017, https://everydayediths.wordpress.com/2017/08/24/3-lessons-on-friendship-from-ruth-naomi.

DR. DHARIUS DANIELS

SPIRITUAL LEADER.
CULTURAL ARCHITECT.
GENERATIONAL TRENDSETTER.

DHARIUSDANIELS.COM | LIFECHANGE.ORG